CRIMINAL JUSTICE TODAY

SPECIAL 1997–98 SUPPLEMENT

FRANK SCHMALLEGER, Ph.D.

The Justice Research Association

Prentice Hall
Upper Saddle River, New Jersey 07458

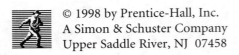 © 1998 by Prentice-Hall, Inc.
A Simon & Schuster Company
Upper Saddle River, NJ 07458

Printed in the United States of America
10 9 8 7 6 5 4 3 2 1

ISBN 0-13-766999-2

PRENTICE-HALL INTERNATIONAL (UK) LIMITED, London
PRENTICE-HALL OF AUSTRALIA PTY. LIMITED, Sydney
PRENTICE-HALL CANADA INC., Toronto
PRENTICE-HALL HISPANOAMERICANA, S.A., Mexico
PRENTICE-HALL OF INDIA PRIVATE LIMITED, New Delhi
PRENTICE-HALL OF JAPAN, INC., Tokyo
SIMON & SCHUSTER ASIA PTE. LTD., Singapore
EDITORA PRENTICE-HALL DO BRASIL, LTDA., Rio de Janeiro

CONTENTS

INTRODUCTION

A year can be a long time. In the 12 months since the fourth edition of *Criminal Justice Today* made its appearance a number of events significant for the study of criminal justice have occurred. New media-magnified crimes (the JonBenet Ramsey murder, for example), significant new trials (i.e., the Timothy McVeigh trial, the O.J. Simpson civil case), noteworthy new U.S. Supreme Court decisions, and new laws (the federal Communications Decency Act, and the Prison Litigation Reform Act), are now all a part of the contemporary scene. Each can serve as an important topic for discussion in criminal justice classrooms.

This special supplement to *Criminal Justice Today* provides an update which students of criminal justice should find especially useful. It begins with a summary of more than a dozen significant U.S. Supreme Court cases (via the Court's Reporter of Decisions syllabi) rendered during the past year, and moves on to provide an overview of important new federal legislation. This supplement concludes with a summary of a new study on the effectiveness of criminal justice research—a study some are calling "the most important study of criminal justice programs ever." Other useful updates can be found at the *Criminal Justice Today* web site, http://www.prenhall.com/cjtoday, and instructors using *Criminal Justice Today* in their classrooms can sign up to receive daily via e-mail the latest news stories about criminal justice happenings by visiting the Simon and Schuster NewsLink website at http://www.ssnewslink.com and clicking on "subscribe." You may also want to contact your Prentice Hall textbook representative to see if you qualify for a NewsLink gift subscription. NewsLink articles are provided to all faculty using *Criminal Justice Today*, upon request.

UPDATES: U.S. SUPREME COURT DECISIONS

SUPREME COURT OF THE UNITED STATES

Syllabus

BOARD OF THE COUNTY COMMISSIONERS OF BRYAN COUNTY, OKLAHOMA *v.* BROWN, et al.

CERTIORARI TO THE UNITED STATES COURT OF APPEALS FOR THE FIFTH CIRCUIT

No. 95–1100. Argued November 5, 1996—Decided April 28, 1997

Respondent brought this 42 U.S.C. Sect. 1983 damages action against petitioner county, alleging, among other things, that its Deputy Burns had arrested her with excessive force, and that it was liable for her injuries because its Sheriff Moore had hired Burns without adequately reviewing his background. Burns had pleaded guilty to various driving infractions and other misdemeanors, including assault and battery. Moore, whom the county stipulated was its Sheriff's Department policymaker, testified that he had obtained Burns' driving and criminal records, but had not closely reviewed either before hiring Burns. The District Court denied the county's motions for judgment as a matter of law, which asserted that a policymaker's single hiring decision could not give rise to Sect. 1983 municipal liability. Respondent prevailed following a jury trial, and the Fifth Circuit affirmed, holding that the county was properly found liable based on Moore's decision to hire Burns.

Held: The county is not liable for Sheriff Moore's isolated decision to hire Burns without adequate screening, because respondent has not demonstrated that the decision reflected a conscious disregard for a high risk that Burns would use excessive force in violation of respondent's federally protected right. Pp. 4–16.

(a) A municipality may not be held liable under Sect. 1983 solely because it employs a tortfeasor, see, e.g., *Monell* v. *New York City Dept. of Social Servs.*, 436 U.S. 658, 692. Instead, the plaintiff must identify a municipal "policy" or "custom" that caused the injury. See, e.g., *Pembaur* v. *Cincinnati*, 475 U.S. 469, 480-481. Contrary to respondent's contention, a "policy" giving rise to liability cannot be established merely by identifying a policymaker's conduct that is properly attributable to the municipality. The plaintiff must also demonstrate that, through its deliberate conduct, the municipality was the "moving force" behind the injury alleged. See *Monell*, supra, at 694. That is, a plaintiff must show that the municipal action was taken with the requisite degree of culpability and must demonstrate a direct causal link between the municipal action and the deprivation of federal rights. Pp. 4–6.

(b) Respondent's claim that a policymaker's single facially lawful hiring decision can trigger municipal liability presents difficult problems of proof. This Court has recognized a Sect. 1983 cause of action based on a single decision attributable to a municipality only where the evidence that the municipality had acted and that the plaintiff had suffered a deprivation of federal rights also proved fault and causation. See, e.g., *Pembaur*, supra, at 481. In relying heavily on *Pembaur*, respondent blurs the distinction between Sect. 1983 cases that present no difficult fault and causation questions and those that do. Claims such as the present, which do not involve an allegation that the municipal action itself violated federal law or directed or authorized the deprivation of federal rights, require application of rigorous culpability and causation standards in order to ensure that the municipality is not held liable solely for its employees' actions. In *Canton* v. *Harris,* 489 U.S. 378, for example, the Court held that a plaintiff seeking to establish municipal liability on the theory that a facially lawful municipal action—there, an allegedly inadequate training program—has led an employee to violate a plaintiff's rights must demonstrate that the municipal action was not simply negligent, but was taken with "deliberate indifference" as to its known or obvious consequences. Id., at 388. Respondent's reliance on *Canton* for an analogy between failure to train cases and inadequate screening cases is not persuasive. In leaving open the possibility that municipal liability could be triggered by evidence of a single violation of federal rights, accompanied by a showing that the municipality has failed to train its employees to handle recurring situations presenting an obvious potential for such a violation, id., at 390, and n. 10, the *Canton* Court simply hypothesized that, in this narrow range of circumstances, the violation may be a highly predictable consequence of the failure to train and thereby justify a finding of "deliberate indifference" by policymakers. Predicting the consequence of a single hiring decision, even one based on an inadequate assessment of a record, is far more difficult. Only where adequate scrutiny of the applicant's background would lead a reasonable policymaker to conclude that the plainly obvious consequence of the decision to hire the applicant would be the deprivation of a third party's federally protected right can the official's failure to adequately scrutinize the applicant's background constitute "deliberate indifference." Neither the District Court nor the Court of Appeals directly tested whether Burns' background made his use of excessive force in making an arrest a plainly obvious consequence of the hiring decision. Pp. 6–14.

(c) Even assuming without deciding that proof of a single instance of inadequate screening could ever trigger municipal liability, Moore's failure to scrutinize Burns' record cannot constitute "deliberate indifference" to respondent's federally protected right to be free from the use of excessive force. To test the link between Moore's action and respondent's injury, it must be asked whether a full review of Burns' record reveals that Moore should have concluded that Burns' use of excessive force would be a plainly obvious consequence of his decision to hire Burns. Respondent's showing on this point was inadequate because the primary infractions on which she relies to prove Burns' propensity for violence arose from a single college fight. A full review of Burns' record might well have led Moore to conclude that Burns was an extremely poor deputy candidate, but he would not necessarily have reached that decision because Burns' use of excessive force would have been a plainly obvious consequence of the decision to hire him. The District Court therefore erred in submitting the inadequate screening theory to the jury. Pp. 14–17.

67 F. 3d 1174, vacated and remanded.

O'Connor, J., delivered the opinion of the Court, in which Rehnquist, C. J., and Scalia, Kennedy, and Thomas, JJ., joined. Souter, J., filed a dissenting opinion, in which Stevens and Breyer, JJ., joined. Breyer, J., filed a dissenting opinion, in which Stevens and Ginsburg, JJ., joined.

SUPREME COURT OF THE UNITED STATES

Syllabus

RICHARDS *v.* WISCONSIN

CERTIORARI TO THE COURT OF SPECIAL APPEALS OF MARYLAND

No. 96–5955. Argued March 24, 1997—Decided April 28, 1997

In *Wilson* v. *Arkansas,* 514 U.S. 927, this Court held that the Fourth Amendment incorporates the common law requirement that police knock on a dwelling's door and announce their identity and purpose before attempting forcible entry, recognized that the flexible reasonableness requirement should not be read to mandate a rigid announcement rule that ignores countervailing law enforcement interests, id., at 934, and left it to the lower courts to determine the circumstances under which an unannounced entry is reasonable. Id., at 936. Officers in Madison, Wisconsin obtained a warrant to search petitioner Richards' hotel room for drugs and related paraphernalia, but the magistrate refused to give advance authorization for a "no knock" entry. The officer who knocked on Richards' door was dressed, and identified himself, as a maintenance man. Upon opening the door, Richards also saw a uniformed officer and quickly closed the door. The officers kicked down the door, caught Richards trying to escape, and found cash and cocaine in the bathroom. In denying Richards' motion to suppress the evidence on the ground that the officers did not knock and announce their presence before forcing entry, the trial court found that they could gather from Richards' strange behavior that he might try to destroy evidence or escape and that the drugs' disposable nature further justified their decision not to knock and announce. The State Supreme Court affirmed, concluding that *Wilson* did not preclude the court's pre-*Wilson per se* rule that police officers are never required to knock and announce when executing a search warrant in a felony drug investigation because of the special circumstances of today's drug culture.

Held:

1. The Fourth Amendment does not permit a blanket exception to the knock and announce requirement for felony drug investigations. While the requirement can give way under circumstances presenting a threat of physical violence or where officers believe that evidence would be destroyed if advance notice were given, 514 U. S., at 936, the fact that felony drug investigations may frequently present such circumstances cannot remove from the neutral scrutiny of a reviewing court the reasonableness of the police decision not to knock and announce in a particular case. Creating exceptions to the requirement based on the culture surrounding a general category of criminal behavior presents at least two serious concerns. First, the exception contains considerable overgeneralization that would impermissibly insulate from judicial review cases in which a drug investigation does not pose special risks. Second, creating an exception in one category can, relatively easily, be applied to others. If a per se exception were allowed for each criminal activity category that included a considerable risk of danger to officers or destruction of evidence, the knock and announce requirement would be meaningless. The court confronted with the question in each case has a duty to determine whether the facts and circumstances of the particular entry justified dispensing with the requirement. A "no knock" entry is justified when the police have a reasonable suspicion that knocking and announcing their presence, under the particular circumstances, would be dangerous or futile, or that it would inhibit the effective investigation of the crime. This standard strikes the appropriate balance between the legitimate law enforcement concerns at issue in the execution of search warrants and the individual privacy interests affected by no knock entries. Cf. *Maryland* v. *Buie*, 494 U.S. 325, 337. Pp. 5–9.

2. Because the evidence in this case establishes that the decision not to knock and announce was a reasonable one under the circumstances, the officers' entry into the hotel room did not violate the Fourth Amendment. That the magistrate had originally refused to issue a no knock warrant means only that at the time the warrant was requested there was insufficient evidence for a no knock entry. However, the officers' decision to enter the room must be evaluated as of the time of entry. Pp. 9–11. 201 Wis. 2d 845, 549 N. W. 2d 218, affirmed.

Stevens, J., delivered the opinion for a unanimous Court.

SUPREME COURT OF THE UNITED STATES

Syllabus

YOUNG, et al. *v.* HARPER

CERTIORARI TO THE UNITED STATES COURT OF APPEALS FOR THE TENTH CIRCUIT

No. 95–1598. Argued December 9, 1996—Decided March 18, 1997

Oklahoma's Preparole Conditional Supervision Program (preparole or Program) took effect whenever the state prisons became overcrowded and authorized the conditional release of prisoners before their sentences expired. The Pardon and Parole Board determined who could participate in it, and an inmate could be placed on preparole after serving 15% of his sentence. An inmate was eligible for parole only after one-third of his sentence had elapsed, and the Governor, based on the Board's recommendation, decided to grant parole. Program participants and parolees were released subject to similar constraints. Upon reviewing respondent's criminal record and prison conduct, the Board simultaneously recommended him for parole and released him under the Program. At that time, he had served 15 years of a life sentence. After he spent five apparently uneventful months outside the penitentiary, the Governor denied him parole, whereupon he was ordered to, and did, report back to prison. Despite his claim that his summary reincarceration deprived him of liberty without due process in violation of the Fourteenth Amendment, he was denied habeas relief by, successively, the state trial court, the Oklahoma Court of Criminal Appeals, and the Federal District Court. The Tenth Circuit reversed, holding that preparole was sufficiently like parole that a Program participant was entitled to the procedural protections set forth in *Morrissey* v. *Brewer*, 408 U. S. 471.

Held: The Program, as it existed when respondent was released, was equivalent to parole as understood in *Morrissey*. *Morrissey's* description of the "nature of the interest of the parolee in his continued liberty" could just as easily have applied to respondent while he was on preparole. In compliance with state procedures, he was released from prison before the expiration of his sentence. See 408 U. S., at 477. He kept his own residence; he sought, obtained, and maintained a job; and he lived a life generally free of the incidents of imprisonment. See *id.,* at 481–482. Although he was not permitted to use alcohol, to incur other than educational debt, or to travel outside the county without permission, and he was required to report regularly to a parole officer, similar limits on a parolee's liberty did not in *Morrissey* render such liberty beyond procedural protection. *Id.,* at 478. Some of the factors asserted by petitioners to differentiate the Program from parole under *Meachum* v. *Fano,* 427 U. S. 215, 228—that preparole had the purpose of reducing prison overcrowding, and that a preparolee continued to serve his sentence and receive earned credits, remained within the custody of the Department of Corrections, and was aware that he could have been transferred to a higher security level if the Governor denied parole—do not, in fact, appear to distinguish the two programs at all. Other differences identified by petitioners—that participation in the Program was ordered by the Board, while the Governor conferred parole; that escaped preparolees could be prosecuted as though they had escaped from prison, while escaped parolees were subject only to parole revocation, and that a preparolee could not leave Oklahoma under any circumstances, while a parolee could leave the State with his parole officer's permission—serve only to set preparole apart from the specific terms of parole as it existed in Oklahoma, but not from the more general class of parole identified in *Morrissey*. The Program appears to have differed from parole in name alone. Pp. 4–9.

64 F. 3d 563, affirmed.

THOMAS, J., delivered the opinion for a unanimous Court.

SUPREME COURT OF THE UNITED STATES

Syllabus

MARYLAND *v.* WILSON

CERTIORARI TO THE COURT OF SPECIAL APPEALS OF MARYLAND

No. 95–1268. Argued December 11, 1996—Decided February 19, 1997

After stopping a speeding car in which respondent Wilson was a passenger, a Maryland state trooper ordered Wilson out of the car upon noticing his apparent nervousness.

When Wilson exited, a quantity of cocaine fell to the ground. He was arrested and charged with possession of cocaine with intent to distribute. The Baltimore County Circuit Court granted his motion to suppress the evidence, deciding that the trooper's ordering him out of the car constituted an unreasonable seizure under the Fourth Amendment. The Maryland Court of Special Appeals affirmed, holding that the rule of *Pennsylvania* v. *Mimms,* 434 U. S. 106, that an officer may as a matter of course order the driver of a lawfully stopped car to exit his vehicle, does not apply to passengers.

Held: An officer making a traffic stop may order passengers to get out of the car pending completion of the stop. Statements by the Court in *Michigan* v. *Long,* 463 U. S. 1032, 1047–1048 (*Mimms* "held that police may order *persons* out of an automobile during a [traffic] stop" (emphasis added)), and by Justice Powell in *Rakas* v. *Illinois,* 439 U. S. 128, 155, n. 4 (*Mimms* held "that *passengers* . . . have no Fourth Amendment right not to be ordered from their vehicle, once a proper stop is made" (emphasis added)), do not constitute binding precedent, since the former statement was dictum, and the latter was contained in a concurrence. Nevertheless, the *Mimms* rule applies to passengers as well as to drivers. The Court therein explained that the touchstone of Fourth Amendment analysis is the reasonableness of the particular governmental invasion of a citizen's personal security, 434 U. S., at 108–109, and that reasonableness depends on a balance between the public interest and the individual's right to personal security free from arbitrary interference by officers, *id.,* at 109. On the public interest side, the same weighty interest in officer safety is present regardless of whether the occupant of the stopped car is a driver, as in *Mimms,* see *id.,* at 109–110, or a passenger, as here. Indeed, the danger to an officer from a traffic stop is likely to be greater when there are passengers in addition to the driver in the stopped car. On the personal liberty side, the case for passengers is stronger than that for the driver in the sense that there is probable cause to believe that the driver has committed a minor vehicular offense, see *id.,* at 110, but there is no such reason to stop or detain passengers. But as a practical matter, passengers are already stopped by virtue of the stop of the vehicle, so that the additional intrusion upon them is minimal. Pp. 2–6.

106 Md. App. 24, 664 A. 2d 1, reversed and remanded.

REHNQUIST, C. J., delivered the opinion of the Court, in which O'CONNOR, SCALIA, SOUTER, THOMAS, GINSBURG, and BREYER, JJ., joined. STEVENS, J., filed a dissenting opinion, in which KENNEDY, J., joined. KENNEDY, J., filed a dissenting opinion.

SUPREME COURT OF THE UNITED STATES

Syllabus

FELKER *v.* TURPIN, WARDEN

CERTIORARI TO THE UNITED STATES COURT OF APPEALS FOR THE ELEVENTH CIRCUIT

No. 95–8836 (A-890). Argued June 3, 1996—Decided June 28, 1996

After he was convicted of murder and other crimes and sentenced to death by a Georgia state court, petitioner was denied relief on direct appeal, in two rounds of state collateral proceedings, and in a first round of federal *habeas corpus* proceedings. While he was awaiting execution, the President signed into law the Antiterrorism and Effective Death Penalty Act of 1996 (Act), Title I of which, as here pertinent, requires dismissal of a claim presented in a state prisoner's second or successive federal habeas application if the claim was also presented in a prior application, §106(b)(1); compels dismissal of a claim that was not presented in a prior federal application, unless certain conditions apply, §106(b)(2); creates a "gatekeeping" mechanism, whereby the prospective applicant files in the court of appeals a motion for leave to file a second or successive habeas application in the district court, and a three-judge panel determines whether the application makes a prima facie showing that it satisfies §106(b)'s requirements, §106(b)(3); and declares that a panel's grant or denial of authorization to file "shall not be appealable and shall not be the subject of a petition for . . . writ of certiorari," §106(b)(3)(E). Petitioner filed a motion for leave to file a second federal habeas petition, which the Eleventh Circuit denied on the grounds, *inter alia,* that the claims to be raised therein had not been presented in his first petition and did not meet §106(b)(2)'s conditions. Petitioner then filed in this Court a pleading styled a "Petition for Writ of *Habeas Corpus* [and] for Appellate or Certiorari Review . . . ." The Court granted certiorari, ordering briefing on the extent to which Title I's provisions apply to a habeas petition filed in this Court, whether application of the Act suspended habeas in this case, and whether Title I, especially §106(b)(3)(E), unconstitutionally restricts the Court's jurisdiction.

Held:

1. The Act does not preclude this Court from entertaining an application for *habeas corpus* relief, although it does affect the standards governing the granting of such relief. Pp. 5–10.

    (a) Title I does not deprive this Court of jurisdiction to entertain habeas petitions filed as original matters pursuant to 28 U. S. C. §§2241 and 2254. No Title I provision mentions the Court's authority to entertain such original petitions; in contrast, §103 amends the Federal Rules of Appellate Procedure to bar consideration of original habeas petitions in the courts of appeals. Although §106(b)(3)(E) precludes the Court from reviewing, by appeal or certiorari, the latter courts' decisions exercising the "gatekeeping" function for second habeas petitions, it makes no mention of the Court's original habeas jurisdiction. Thus, the Court declines to find a repeal of §2241 by implication. See *Ex parte Yerger,* 8 Wall. 85, 105. This conclusion obviates any claim by petitioner under the Constitution's Exceptions Clause, Art. III, §2, which provides, *inter alia,* that, "[i]n all . . . Cases . . . the Supreme Court shall have appellate Jurisdiction, both as to Law and Fact, with such Exceptions . . . as the Congress shall make." Since the Act does not repeal the Court's authority to entertain a habeas petition, there can be no plausible argument that it deprives the Court of appellate jurisdiction in violation of that Clause. Pp. 6–9.

    (b) Title I changes the standards governing this Court's consideration of habeas petitions by imposing new requirements under 28 U. S. C. §2254(a), which limits the Court's authority to grant relief to state prisoners. Section 106(b)(3)'s "gatekeeping" system does not apply to the Court because it is limited to applications "filed in the district court." There is no such limitation, however, on the restrictions imposed by §§106(b)(1) and (2), and those restrictions inform the Court's authority to grant relief on original habeas petitions, whether or not the Court is bound by the restrictions. Pp. 9–10.

2. The Act does not violate the Constitution's Suspension Clause, Art. I, §9, cl. 2, which provides that "[t]he Privilege of the Writ of *Habeas Corpus* shall not be suspended." The new restrictions on successive habeas petitions constitute a modified *res judicata* rule, a restraint on what is called in habeas practice "abuse of the writ." The doctrine of abuse of the writ refers to a complex and evolving body of equitable principles

informed and controlled by historical usage, statutory developments, and judicial decisions. *McCleskey* v. *Zant,* 499 U. S. 467, 489. The new restrictions are well within the compass of this evolutionary process and do not amount to a "suspension" of the writ. Pp. 10–12.

3. The petition for an original writ of *habeas corpus* is denied. Petitioner's claims do not satisfy the §106(b)(2) requirements, let alone this Court's Rule 20.4(a), which requires that the habeas petitioner show "exceptional circumstances" justifying the issuance of the writ and says that habeas relief is rarely granted. Petitioner's claims here do not materially differ from numerous other claims made by successive habeas petitioners that the Court has had occasion to review on stay applications. P. 12.

Certiorari dismissed for want of jurisdiction; writ of *habeas corpus* denied.

REHNQUIST, C. J., delivered the opinion for a unanimous Court. STEVENS, J., filed a concurring opinion, in which SOUTER and BREYER, JJ., joined. SOUTER, J., filed a concurring opinion, in which STEVENS and BREYER, JJ., joined.

SUPREME COURT OF THE UNITED STATES

Syllabus

UNITED STATES *v.* URSERY

CERTIORARI TO THE UNITED STATES COURT OF APPEALS FOR THE SIXTH CIRCUIT

No. 95–345. Argued April 17, 1996—Decided June 24, 1996

In No. 95–345, the Government instituted civil forfeiture proceedings under 21 U. S. C. §881(a)(7) against respondent Ursery's house, alleging that it had been used to facilitate illegal drug transactions. Shortly before Ursery settled that claim, he was indicted, and was later convicted, of manufacturing marijuana in violation of §841(a)(1). In No. 95-346, the Government filed a civil in rem complaint against various property seized from, or titled to, respondents Arlt and Wren or Arlt's corporation, alleging that each item was subject to forfeiture under 18 U. S. C. §981(a)(1)(A) because it was involved in money laundering violative of §1956, and to forfeiture under 21 U. S. C. §881(a)(6) as the proceeds of a felonious drug transaction. Litigation of the forfeiture action was deferred while Arlt and Wren were prosecuted on drug and money-laundering charges under §846 and 18 U. S. C. §§371 and 1956. After their convictions, the District Court granted the Government's motion for summary judgment in the forfeiture proceeding. The Courts of Appeals reversed Ursery's conviction and the forfeiture judgment against Arlt and Wren, holding that the Double Jeopardy Clause prohibits the Government from both punishing a defendant for a criminal offense and forfeiting his property for that same offense in a separate civil proceeding. The courts reasoned in part that *Halper* v. *United States,* 490 U. S. 435, and *Austin* v. *United States,* 509 U. S. 602, meant that, as a categorical matter, civil forfeitures always constitute "punishment" for double jeopardy purposes. This Court consolidated the cases.

Held: In rem civil forfeitures are neither "punishment" nor criminal for purposes of the Double Jeopardy Clause. Pp. 3-23.

(a) Congress long has authorized the Government to bring parallel criminal actions and *in rem* civil forfeiture proceedings based upon the same underlying events, see, *e.g.,*

The Palmyra, 12 Wheat. 1, 14–15, and this Court consistently has concluded that the Double Jeopardy Clause does not apply to such forfeitures because they do not impose punishment, see, *e.g., Various Items of Personal Property* v. *United States,* 282 U. S. 577, 581; *One Lot Emerald Cut Stones* v. *United States,* 409 U. S. 232, 235–236 (*per curiam*). In its most recent case, *United States* v. *One Assortment of 89 Firearms,* 465 U. S. 354, the Court held that a forfeiture was not barred by a prior criminal proceeding after applying a two-part test asking, first, whether Congress intended the particular forfeiture to be a remedial civil sanction or a criminal penalty, and, second, whether the forfeiture proceedings are so punitive in fact as to establish that they may not legitimately be viewed as civil in nature, despite any congressional intent to establish a civil remedial mechanism. Pp. 5–9.

(b) Though the *89 Firearms* test was more refined, perhaps, than the Court's *Various Items* analysis, the conclusion was the same in each case: *in rem* civil forfeiture is a remedial civil sanction, distinct from potentially punitive *in personam* civil penalties such as fines, and does not constitute a punishment for double jeopardy purposes. See *Gore* v. *United States,* 357 U. S. 386, 392. The Courts of Appeals misread *Halper, Austin,* and *Montana Dept. of Revenue* v. *Kurth Ranch,* 511 U. S. ___, as having abandoned this oft-affirmed rule. None of those decisions purported to overrule *Various Items, Emerald Cut Stones,* and *89 Firearms* or to replace the Court's traditional understanding. It would have been remarkable for the Court both to have held unconstitutional a well-established practice, and to have overruled a long line of precedent, without having even suggested that it was doing so. Moreover, the cases in question did not deal with the subject of this case: *in rem* civil forfeitures for double jeopardy purposes. *Halper* involved *in personam* civil penalties under the Double Jeopardy Clause. *Kurth Ranch* considered a punitive state tax imposed on marijuana under that Clause. And *Austin* dealt with civil forfeitures under the Eighth Amendment's Excessive Fines Clause. Pp. 10–19.

(c) The forfeitures at issue are civil proceedings under the two-part *89 Firearms* test. First, there is little doubt that Congress intended proceedings under §§881 and 981 to be civil, since those statutes' procedural enforcement mechanisms are themselves distinctly civil in nature. See, *e.g., 89 Firearms,* 465 U. S., at 363. Second, there is little evidence, much less the "clearest proof" that the Court requires, see *e.g., id.,* at 365, suggesting that forfeiture proceedings under those sections are so punitive in form and effect as to render them criminal despite Congress' intent to the contrary. These statutes are, in most significant respects, indistinguishable from those reviewed, and held not to be punitive, in *Various Items, Emerald Cut Stones,* and *89 Firearms.* That these are civil proceedings is also supported by other factors that the Court has found persuasive, including the considerations that (1) *in rem* civil forfeiture has not historically been regarded as punishment; (2) there is no requirement in the statutes at issue that the Government demonstrate *scienter* in order to establish that the property is subject to forfeiture; (3) though both statutes may serve a deterrent purpose, this purpose may serve civil as well as criminal goals; and (4) the fact that both are tied to criminal activity is insufficient in itself to render them punitive. See, *e.g., United States* v. *Ward,* 448 U. S. 242, 247–248, n. 7, 249. Pp. 19–23.

No. 95–345, 59 F. 3d 568, and No. 95–346, 33 F. 3d 1210 and 56 F. 3d 41, reversed.

REHNQUIST, C. J., delivered the opinion of the Court, in which O'CONNOR, KENNEDY, SOUTER, GINSBURG, and BREYER, JJ., joined. KENNEDY, J., filed a concurring opinion. SCALIA, J., filed an opinion concurring in the judgment, in which THOMAS, J., joined. STEVENS, J., filed an opinion concurring in the judgment in part and dissenting in part.

SUPREME COURT OF THE UNITED STATES

Syllabus

LEWIS, DIRECTOR, ARIZONA DEPARTMENT OF CORRECTIONS, et al.
v. CASEY et al.

CERTIORARI TO THE UNITED STATES COURT OF APPEALS FOR THE NINTH CIRCUIT

No. 94–1511. Argued November 29, 1995—Decided June 24, 1996

Respondents, who are inmates of various prisons operated by the Arizona Department of Corrections (ADOC), brought a class action against petitioners, ADOC officials, alleging that petitioners were furnishing them with inadequate legal research facilities and thereby depriving them of their right of access to the courts, in violation of *Bounds* v. *Smith,* 430 U. S. 817. The District Court found petitioners to be in violation of *Bounds* and issued an injunction mandating detailed, systemwide changes in ADOC's prison law libraries and in its legal assistance programs. The Ninth Circuit affirmed both the finding of a *Bounds* violation and the injunction's major terms.

Held: The success of respondents' systemic challenge was dependent on their ability to show widespread actual injury, and the District Court's failure to identify anything more than isolated instances of actual injury renders its finding of a systemic *Bounds* violation invalid. Pp. 3–20.

(a) *Bounds* did not create an abstract, free-standing right to a law library or legal assistance; rather, the right that *Bounds* acknowledged was the right of *access to the courts. E.g.,* 430 U. S., at 817, 821, 828. Thus, to establish a *Bounds* violation, the "actual injury" that an inmate must demonstrate is that the alleged shortcomings in the prison library or legal assistance program have hindered, or are presently hindering, his efforts to pursue a non-frivolous legal claim. This requirement derives ultimately from the doctrine of standing. Although *Bounds* made no mention of an actual injury requirement, it can hardly be thought to have eliminated that constitutional prerequisite. Pp. 4–9.

(b) Statements in *Bounds* suggesting that prison authorities must also enable the prisoner to *discover* grievances, and to *litigate effectively* once in court, *id.,* at 825–826, and n. 14, have no antecedent in this Court's pre-*Bounds* cases, and are now disclaimed. Moreover, *Bounds* does not guarantee inmates the wherewithal to file any and every type of legal claim, but requires only that they be provided with the tools to attack their sentences, directly or collaterally, and to challenge the conditions of their confinement. Pp. 9–11.

(c) The District Court identified only two instances of actual injury: It found that ADOC's failures with respect to illiterate prisoners had resulted in the dismissal with prejudice of inmate Bartholic's lawsuit and the inability of inmate Harris to file a legal action. Pp. 11–12.

(d) These findings as to injury do not support the systemwide injunction ordered by the District Court. The remedy must be limited to the inadequacy that produced the injury-in-fact that the plaintiff has established; that this is a class action changes nothing, for even named plaintiffs in a class action must show that they personally have been injured, see, *e.g., Simon* v. *Eastern Ky. Welfare Rights Organization,* 426 U. S. 26, 40, n. 20. Only one named plaintiff, Bartholic, was found to have suffered actual injury—as a result of ADOC's failure to provide the special services he would have needed, in light of his particular disability (illiteracy), to avoid dismissal of his case. Eliminated from the proper scope of the injunction, therefore, are provisions directed at special services or facilities required by non-English-speakers, by prisoners in lockdown, and by the inmate population at large. Furthermore, the inadequacy that caused actual injury to illiterate inmates Bartholic and Harris was not sufficiently widespread to justify systemwide relief. There is no finding, and no evidence discernible from the record, that in ADOC prisons other than those occupied by Bartholic and Harris illiterate inmates cannot obtain the minimal help necessary to file legal claims. Pp. 12–16.

(e) There are further reasons why the order here cannot stand. In concluding that ADOC's restrictions on lockdown inmates were unjustified, the District Court failed to accord the judgment of prison authorities the substantial deference required by cases such as *Turner* v. *Safley,* 482 U. S. 78, 89. The court also failed to leave with prison officials the primary responsibility for devising a remedy. Compare *Preiser* v. *Rodriguez,* 411 U. S. 475, 492. The result of this improper procedure was an inordinately intrusive order. Pp. 17–20.

43 F. 3d 1261, reversed and remanded.

SCALIA, J., delivered the opinion of the Court, in which REHNQUIST, C. J., and O'CONNOR, KENNEDY, and THOMAS, JJ., joined, and in Parts I and III of which SOUTER, GINSBURG, and BREYER, JJ., joined. THOMAS, J., filed a concurring opinion. SOUTER, J., filed an opinion concurring in part, dissenting in part, and concurring in the judgment, in which GINSBURG and BREYER, JJ., joined. STEVENS, J., filed a dissenting opinion.

S U P R E M E   C O U R T
O F   T H E   U N I T E D   S T A T E S

Syllabus

MELENDEZ *v.* UNITED STATES

CERTIORARI TO THE UNITED STATES COURT OF APPEALS FOR THE THIRD CIRCUIT

No. 95–5661. Argued February 27, 1996—Decided June 17, 1996

After agreeing with others to buy cocaine, petitioner was charged with a conspiracy violative of 21 U. S. C. §846, which carries a statutory minimum sentence of 10 years' imprisonment. He ultimately signed a plea agreement providing, *inter alia,* that in return for his cooperation with the Government's investigation and his guilty plea, the Government would move the sentencing court, pursuant to §5K1.1 of the United States Sentencing Guidelines, to depart downward from the otherwise applicable Guideline sentencing range, which turned out to be 135-to-168 months' imprisonment. Although the agreement noted the applicability of the 10-year statutory minimum sentence, neither it nor the ensuing §5K1.1 motion mentioned departure below that minimum. Pursuant to the motion, the District Court departed downward from the Guideline range in sentencing petitioner. It also ruled, however, that it had no authority to depart below the statutory minimum because the Government had not made a motion, pursuant 18 U. S. C. §3553(e), that it do so. It thus sentenced petitioner to 10 years, and the Third Circuit affirmed.

Held: A Government motion attesting to the defendant's substantial assistance in a criminal investigation and requesting that the district court depart below the minimum of the applicable Guideline sentencing range does not also authorize the court to depart below a lower statutory minimum sentence. Pp. 3–11.

(a) Guideline §5K1.1 does not create a "unitary" motion system. Title 18 U. S. C. §3553(e) requires a Government motion requesting or authorizing the district court to "impose a sentence below a level established by statute as minimum sentence" before the court may impose such a sentence. Nothing in §3553(e) suggests that a district court has the power to impose such a sentence when the Government has not authorized it, but has instead moved for a departure only from the applicable Guidelines range. Nor does anything in §3553(e) or 28 U. S. C. §994(n) suggest that the Commission itself may dispense with §3553(e)'s motion requirement, or alternatively, "deem" a motion requesting or authorizing different action— such as a departure below the Guidelines minimum—to be a motion authorizing departure below the statutory minimum. Section 5K1.1 cannot be read as attempting to exercise this nonexistent authority. That section states that, "[u]pon motion of the government . . . the court may depart from the guidelines," while its Application Note 1 declares that, "[u]nder circumstances set forth in . . . §3553(e) and . . . §994(n) . . . substantial assistance . . . may justify a sentence below a statutorily required minimum sentence." One of the circumstances set forth in §3553(e) is that the Government has authorized the court to impose such a sentence. The Government is correct that the relevant statutory provisions merely charge the Commission with constraining the district court's discretion in choosing a specific sentence once the Government has moved for a departure below the statutory minimum, not with "implementing" §3553(e)'s motion requirement, and that §5K1.1 does not improperly attempt to dispense with or modify that requirement. Pp. 3–10.

(b) For two reasons, the Court need not decide whether the Government is correct in reading §994(n) to permit the Commission to construct a unitary motion system by providing that the district court may depart below the Guidelines range only when the Government is willing to authorize the court to depart below the statutory minimum, if the court finds that to be appropriate. First, even if the Commission had done so, that would not help petitioner, since the Government has not authorized a departure below the statutory minimum here. Second, the Commission has not adopted this type of unitary system. Pp. 10–11.

55 F. 3d 130, affirmed.

THOMAS, J., delivered the opinion of the Court, in which REHNQUIST, C. J., and SCALIA, KENNEDY, SOUTER, and GINSBURG, JJ., joined, and in which O'CONNOR and BREYER, JJ., joined as to Parts I and II. SOUTER, J., filed a concurring opinion. STEVENS, J., filed an opinion concurring in the judgment. BREYER, J., filed an opinion concurring in part and dissenting in part, in which O'CONNOR, J., joined.

SUPREME COURT
OF THE UNITED STATES

Syllabus

MONTANA *v.* EGELHOFF

CERTIORARI TO THE SUPREME COURT OF MONTANA

No. 95–566. Argued March 20, 1996—Decided June 13, 1996

On trial for two counts of deliberate homicide—defined by Montana law as "purposely" or "knowingly" causing another's death—respondent claimed that extreme intoxication had rendered him physically incapable of committing the murders and accounted for his inability to recall the events of the night in question. After being instructed, pursuant to

Mont. Code Ann. §45–2–203, that respondent's "intoxicated condition" could not be considered "in determining the existence of a mental state which is an element of the offense," the jury found respondent guilty. In reversing, the Supreme Court of Montana reasoned that respondent had a right, under the Due Process Clause, to present and have the jury consider "all relevant evidence" to rebut the State's evidence on all elements of the offense charged, and that evidence of his voluntary intoxication was "clearly relevant" to the issue whether he acted knowingly and purposely. Because §45–2–203 prevented the jury from considering that evidence, the court concluded that the State had been relieved of part of its burden of proof and that respondent had therefore been denied due process.

Held: The judgment is reversed.

272 Mont. 114, 900 P. 2d 260, reversed.

JUSTICE SCALIA, joined by THE CHIEF JUSTICE, JUSTICE KENNEDY, and JUSTICE THOMAS, concluded that §45–2–203 does not violate the Due Process Clause. Pp. 3–19.

(a) The State Supreme Court's proposition that the Due Process Clause guarantees the right to introduce *all relevant evidence* is indefensible. See, *e.g., Taylor* v. *Illinois,* 484 U. S. 400, 410; Fed. Rule Evid. 403; Fed. Rule Evid. 802. The Clause does place limits upon restriction of the right to introduce evidence, but only where the restriction "offends some principle of justice so rooted in the traditions and conscience of our people as to be ranked as fundamental." See *Patterson* v. *New York,* 432 U. S. 197, 201–202. Respondent has failed to meet the heavy burden of establishing that a defendant's right to have a jury consider voluntary intoxication evidence in determining whether he possesses the requisite mental state is a "fundamental principle of justice." The primary guide in making such a determination, historical practice, gives respondent little support. It was firmly established at common law that a defendant's voluntary intoxication provided neither an "excuse" nor a "justification" for his crimes; the common law's stern rejection of inebriation as a defense must be understood as also precluding a defendant from arguing that, because of his intoxication, he could not have possessed the *mens rea* necessary to commit the crime. The justifications for this common-law rule persist to this day, and have only been strengthened by modern research. Although a rule allowing a jury to consider evidence of a defendant's voluntary intoxication where relevant to *mens rea* has gained considerable acceptance since the 19th century, it is of too recent vintage, and has not received sufficiently uniform and permanent allegiance to qualify as fundamental, especially since it displaces a lengthy common-law tradition which remains supported by valid justifications. Pp. 3–13.

(b) None of this Court's cases on which the Supreme Court of Montana's conclusion purportedly rested undermines the principle that a State can limit the introduction of relevant evidence for a "valid" reason, as Montana has. The Due Process Clause does not bar States from making changes in their criminal law that have the effect of making it easier for the prosecution to obtain convictions. See *McMillan* v. *Pennsylvania,* 477 U. S. 79, 89, n. 5. Pp. 14-19.

JUSTICE GINSBURG concluded that §45–2–203 should not be categorized as simply an evidentiary rule. Rather, §45–2–203 embodies a legislative judgment regarding the circumstances under which individuals may be held criminally responsible for their actions. The provision judges equally culpable a person who commits an act stone sober, and one who engages in the same conduct after voluntary intoxication has reduced the actor's capacity for self-control. Comprehended as a measure redefining *mens rea,* §45–2–203 encounters no constitutional shoal. States have broad authority to define the elements of criminal offenses in light of evolving perceptions of the extent to which moral culpability should be a prerequisite to conviction of a crime. Defining *mens rea* to eliminate the exculpatory value of voluntary intoxication does not offend a fundamen-

tal principle of justice, given the lengthy common-law tradition, and the adherence of a significant minority of the States to that position today. Pp. 1–5.

SCALIA, J., announced the judgment of the Court and delivered an opinion, in which REHNQUIST, C. J., and KENNEDY and THOMAS, JJ., joined. GINSBURG, J., filed an opinion concurring in the judgment. O'CONNOR, J., filed a dissenting opinion, in which STEVENS, SOUTER, and BREYER, JJ., joined. SOUTER, J., filed a dissenting opinion. BREYER, J., filed a dissenting opinion, in which STEVENS, J., joined.

SUPREME COURT OF THE UNITED STATES

Syllabus

KOON *v.* UNITED STATES

CERTIORARI TO THE UNITED STATES COURT OF APPEALS FOR THE NINTH CIRCUIT

No. 94–1664. Argued February 20, 1996—Decided June 13, 1996

After petitioners, Los Angeles police officers, were acquitted on state charges of assault and excessive use of force in the beating of a suspect during an arrest, they were convicted under 18 U. S. C. §242 of violating the victim's constitutional rights under color of law. Although the applicable United States Sentencing Guideline, 1992 USSG §2H1.4, indicated that they should be imprisoned for 70 to 87 months, the District Court granted them two downward departures from that range. The first was based on the victim's misconduct, which contributed significantly to provoking the offense. The second was based on a combination of four factors: (1) that petitioners were unusually susceptible to abuse in prison; (2) that petitioners would lose their jobs and be precluded from employment in law enforcement; (3) that petitioners had been subject to successive state and federal prosecutions; and (4) that petitioners posed a low risk of recidivism. The sentencing range after the departures was 30 to 37 months, and the court sentenced each petitioner to 30 months. The Ninth Circuit reviewed the departure decisions *de novo* and rejected all of them.

Held:

1. An appellate court should not review *de novo* a decision to depart from the Guideline sentencing range, but instead should ask whether the sentencing court abused its discretion. Pp. 8–17.

(a) Although the Sentencing Reform Act of 1984 requires that a district court impose a sentence within the applicable Guideline range in an ordinary case, 18 U. S. C. §3553(a), it does not eliminate all of the district court's traditional sentencing discretion. Rather, it allows a departure from the range if the court finds "there exists an aggravating or mitigating circumstance of a kind, to a degree, not adequately taken into consideration" by the Sentencing Commission in formulating the Guidelines, §3553(b). The Commission states that it has formulated each Guideline to apply to a "heartland" of typical cases and that it did not "adequately . . . conside[r]" atypical cases, 1995 USSG ch. 1, pt. A., intro. comment. 4(b). The Commission prohibits consideration of a few factors, and it provides guidance as to the factors that are likely to make a case atypical by delineating certain of them as "encouraged" bases for departure and others as "discouraged" bases for departure. Courts may depart on the basis of an encouraged factor if the applicable Guideline does not already take the factor into account. A court may depart on the basis of a discouraged factor, or an encouraged factor already taken into account, however, only if the factor is present to an exceptional degree or in some other way makes the case different from the ordinary case. If the Guidelines do not mention a factor, the court must, after considering the structure and theory of relevant individual Guidelines and the Guidelines as a whole, decide whether the factor is sufficiently unusual to take the case out of the Guideline's heartland, bearing in mind the Commission's expectation that departures based on factors not mentioned in the Guidelines will be "highly infrequent." Pp. 8–13.

(b) Although §3742 established a limited appellate review of sentencing decisions, §3742(e)(4)'s direction to "give due deference to the district court's application of the guidelines to the facts" demonstrates that the Act was not intended to vest in appellate courts wide-ranging authority over district court sentencing decisions. See, e.g., *Williams* v. *United States,* 503 U. S. 193, 205. The deference that is due depends on the nature of the question presented. A departure decision will in most cases be due substantial deference, for it embodies the sentencing court's traditional exercise of discretion. See *Mistretta* v. *United States,* 488 U. S. 361, 367. To determine if a departure is appropriate, the district court must make a refined assessment of the many facts that bear on the outcome, informed by its vantage point and day-to-day sentencing experience. Whether a given factor is present to a degree not adequately considered by the Commission, or whether a discouraged factor nonetheless justifies departure because it is present in some unusual or exceptional way, are matters determined in large part by comparison with the facts of other Guidelines cases. District courts have an institutional advantage over appellate courts in making these sorts of determinations, especially given that they see so many more Guidelines cases. Such considerations require adoption of the abuse-of-discretion standard of review, not *de novo* review. See, *e.g., Cooter & Gell* v. *Hartmarx Corp.,* 496 U. S. 384, 403. Pp. 13–17.

2. Because the Court of Appeals erred in rejecting certain of the downward departure factors relied upon by the District Judge, the foregoing principles require reversal of the appellate court's rulings in significant part. Pp. 18–31.

(a) Victim misconduct is an encouraged basis for departure under USSG §5K2.10, and the District Court did not abuse its discretion in basing a departure on it. The court's analysis of this departure factor showed a correct understanding in applying §2H1.4, the Guideline applicable to 18 U. S. C. §242, both as a mechanical matter and in interpreting its heartland. As the court recognized, §2H1.4 incorporates the Guideline for the offense underlying the §242 violation, here §2A2.2 for aggravated assault, and thus creates a Guideline range and a heartland for aggravated assault committed under color of law. A downward departure under §5K2.10 was justified because the punishment prescribed by §2A2.2 contemplates unprovoked assaults, not cases like this where what begins as legitimate force in response to provocation becomes excessive. The Court of Appeals misinterpreted the District Court to have found that the victim had been the but-for cause of the crime, but not that he had provoked it; it also misinterpreted the heartland of the applicable Guideline range by concentrating on whether the victim's misconduct made this an unusual case of excessive force. Pp. 18–23.

(b) This Court rejects the Government's contention that some of the four considerations underlying the District Court's second downward departure are impermissible departure factors under all circumstances. For a court to conclude that a factor must never be considered would be to usurp the policy-making authority that Congress vested in the Commission, and 18 U. S. C. §3553(a)(2) does not compel such a result. A court's examination of whether a factor can ever be an appropriate basis for departure is limited to determining whether the Commission has proscribed, as a categorical matter, that factor's consideration. If the answer is no—as it will be most of the time—the sentencing court must determine whether the factor, as occurring in the particular circumstances, takes the case outside the applicable Guideline's heartland. Pp. 23–26.

(c) The District Court abused its discretion in relying on petitioners' collateral employment consequences as support for its second departure. Because it is to be expected that a public official convicted of using his governmental authority to violate a person's rights will lose his or her job and be barred from similar employment in the future, it must be concluded that the Commission adequately considered these consequences in formulating 1992 USSG §2H1.4. Thus, the career loss factor, as it exists in this case, cannot take the case out of §2H1.4's heartland. Pp. 26–28.

(d) The low likelihood of petitioners' recidivism was also an inappropriate ground for departure, since the Commission specifically addressed this factor in formulating the sentencing range for petitioners' criminal history category. See §4A1.3. Pp. 28–29.

(e) However, the District Court did not abuse its discretion in relying upon susceptibility to abuse in prison and the burdens of successive prosecutions. The District Court's finding that the case is unusual due to petitioners exceptional susceptibility to abuse in prison is just the sort of determination that must be accorded deference on appeal. Moreover, although consideration of petitioners' successive prosecutions could be incongruous with the dual responsibilities of citizenship in our federal system, this Court cannot conclude the District Court abused its discretion by considering that factor. Pp. 29–30.

(f) Where a reviewing court concludes that a district court based a departure on both valid and invalid factors, a remand is required unless the reviewing court determines that the district court would have imposed the same sentence absent reliance on the invalid factors. *Williams, supra,* at 203. Because the District Court here stated that none of four factors standing alone would justify its second departure, it is not evident that the court would have imposed the same sentence had it relied only on susceptibility to abuse and the hardship of successive prosecutions. The Court of Appeals should therefore remand the case to the District Court. Pp. 30–31.

34 F. 3d 1416, affirmed in part, reversed in part, and remanded.

KENNEDY, J., delivered the opinion of the Court, in which REHNQUIST, C. J., and O'CONNOR, SCALIA, and THOMAS, JJ., joined, in all but Part IV–B–1 of which STEVENS, J., joined, and in all but Part IV–B–3 of which SOUTER, GINSBURG, and BREYER, JJ., joined. STEVENS, J., filed an opinion concurring in part and dissenting in part. SOUTER, J. filed an opinion concurring in part and dissenting in part, in which GINSBURG, J., joined. BREYER, J., filed an opinion concurring in part and disenting in part, in which GINSBURG, J., joined.

SUPREME COURT OF THE UNITED STATES

Syllabus

WHREN, et al. *v.* UNITED STATES

CERTIORARI TO THE UNITED STATES COURT OF APPEALS FOR THE DISTRICT OF COLUMBIA CIRCUIT

No. 95–5841. Argued April 17, 1996—Decided June 10, 1996

Plainclothes policemen patrolling a "high drug area" in an unmarked vehicle observed a truck driven by petitioner Brown waiting at a stop sign at an intersection for an unusually long time;

the truck then turned suddenly, without signaling, and sped off at an "unreasonable" speed. The officers stopped the vehicle, assertedly to warn the driver about traffic violations, and upon approaching the truck observed plastic bags of crack cocaine in petitioner Wren's hands. Petitioners were arrested. Prior to trial on federal drug charges, they moved for suppression of the evidence, arguing that the stop had not been justified by either a reasonable suspicion or probable cause to believe petitioners were engaged in illegal drug-dealing activity, and that the officers' traffic-violation ground for approaching the truck was pretextual. The motion to suppress was denied, petitioners were convicted, and the Court of Appeals affirmed.

Held: The temporary detention of a motorist upon probable cause to believe that he has violated the traffic laws does not violate the Fourth Amendment's prohibition against unreasonable seizures, even if a reasonable officer would not have stopped the motorist absent some additional law enforcement objective. Pp. 3–13.

(a) Detention of a motorist is reasonable where probable cause exists to believe that a traffic violation has occurred. See, *e.g., Delaware* v. *Prouse,* 440 U. S. 648, 659. Petitioners claim that, because the police may be tempted to use commonly occurring traffic violations as means of investigating violations of other laws, the Fourth Amendment test for traffic stops should be whether a reasonable officer would have stopped the car for the purpose of enforcing the traffic violation at issue. However, this Court's cases foreclose the argument that ulterior motives can invalidate police conduct justified on the basis of probable cause. See, *e.g., United States* v. *Robinson,* 414 U. S. 218, 221, n. 1, 236. Subjective intentions play no role in ordinary, probable-cause Fourth Amendment analysis. Pp. 3–7.

(b) Although framed as an empirical question—whether the officer's conduct deviated materially from standard police practices—petitioners' proposed test is plainly designed to combat the perceived danger of pretextual stops. It is thus inconsistent with this Court's cases, which make clear that the Fourth Amendment's concern with "reasonableness" allows certain actions to be taken in certain circumstances, *whatever* the subjective intent. See, *e.g., Robinson, supra,* at 236. Nor can the Fourth Amendment's protections be thought to vary from place to place and from time to time, which would be the consequence of assessing the reasonableness of police conduct in light of local law enforcement practices. Pp. 7–10.

(c) Also rejected is petitioners' argument that the balancing of interests inherent in Fourth Amendment inquiries does not support enforcement of minor traffic laws by plainclothes police in unmarked vehicles, since that practice only minimally advances the government's interest in traffic safety while subjecting motorists to inconvenience, confusion, and anxiety. Where probable cause exists, this Court has found it necessary to engage in balancing only in cases involving searches or seizures conducted in a manner unusually harmful to the individual. See, *e.g., Tennessee* v. *Garner,* 471 U. S. 1. The making of a traffic stop out-of-uniform does not remotely qualify as such an extreme practice. Pp. 10–13.

53 F. 3d 371, affirmed.

SCALIA, J., delivered the opinion for a unanimous Court.

SUPREME COURT
OF THE UNITED STATES

Syllabus

ORNELAS, et al. *v.* UNITED STATES

CERTIORARI TO THE UNITED STATES COURT OF APPEALS FOR THE SEVENTH CIRCUIT

No. 95–5257. Argued March 26, 1996-Decided—May 28, 1996

In denying petitioners' motion to suppress cocaine found in their car, the District Court ruled that the police had reasonable suspicion to stop and question petitioners, and probable cause to remove one of the interior panels where a package containing the cocaine was found. The Court of Appeals ultimately affirmed both determinations, reviewing each "deferentially," and "for clear error," and finding no clear error in either instance.

Held: The ultimate questions of reasonable suspicion to stop and probable cause to make a warrantless search should be reviewed *de novo.* The principal components of either inquiry are (1) a determination of the historical facts leading up to the stop or search, and (2) a decision on the mixed question of law and fact whether the historical facts, viewed from the standpoint of an objectively reasonable police officer, amount to reasonable suspicion or to probable cause. Independent appellate review of the latter determination is consistent with the position taken by this Court, see, *e.g., Brinegar* v. *United States,* 338 U. S. 160, 160; will prevent unacceptably varied results based on the interpretation of similar facts by different trial judges, see *id.,* at 171; is necessary if appellate courts are to maintain control of, and to clarify, the pertinent legal rules, see *Miller* v. *Fenton,* 474 U. S. 104, 114; and will tend to unify precedent and to provide police with a defined set of rules which, in most instances, will make it possible to reach a correct determination beforehand as to whether an invasion of privacy is justified in the interest of law enforcement, see, *e.g., New York* v. *Belton,* 453 U. S. 454, 458. However, a reviewing court should take care both to review findings of historical fact only for clear error and to give due weight to inferences drawn therefrom by resident judges, who view such facts in light of the community's distinctive features and events, and by local police, who view the facts through the lens of their experience and expertise. Pp. 5–10.

16 F. 3d 714 and 52 F. 3d 328, vacated and remanded.

REHNQUIST, C. J., delivered the opinion of the Court, in which STEVENS, O'CONNOR, KENNEDY, SOUTER, THOMAS, GINSBURG, and BREYER, JJ., joined. SCALIA, J., filed a dissenting opinion.

SUPREME COURT OF THE UNITED STATES

Syllabus

BMW OF NORTH AMERICA, INC. *v.* GORE

CERTIORARI TO THE SUPREME COURT OF ALABAMA

No. 94–896. Argued October 11, 1995—Decided May 20, 1996

After respondent Gore purchased a new BMW automobile from an authorized Alabama dealer, he discovered that the car had been repainted. He brought this suit for compensatory and punitive damages against petitioner, the American distributor of BMW's, alleging, *inter alia,* that the failure to disclose the repainting constituted fraud under Alabama law. At trial, BMW acknowledged that it followed a nationwide policy of not advising its dealers, and hence their customers, of predelivery damage to new cars when the cost of repair did not exceed 3 percent of the car's suggested retail price. Gore's vehicle fell into that category. The jury returned a verdict finding BMW liable for compensatory damages of $4,000, and assessing $4 million in punitive damages. The trial judge denied BMW's post-trial motion to set aside the punitive damages award, holding, among other things, that the award was not "grossly excessive" and thus did not violate the Due Process Clause of the Fourteenth Amendment. See, *e.g., TXO Production Corp.* v. *Alliance Resources Corp.,* 509 U. S. 443, 454. The Alabama Supreme Court agreed, but reduced the award to $2 million on the ground that, in computing the amount, the jury had improperly multiplied Gore's compensatory damages by the number of similar sales in all States, not just those in Alabama.

Held: The $2 million punitive damages award is grossly excessive and therefore exceeds the constitutional limit. Pp. 7–26.

(a) Because such an award violates due process only when it can fairly be categorized as "grossly excessive" in relation to the State's legitimate interests in punishing unlawful conduct and deterring its repetition, *cf. TXO,* 509 U. S., at 456, the federal excessiveness inquiry appropriately begins with an identification of the state interests that such an award is designed to serve. Principles of state sovereignty and comity forbid a State to enact policies for the entire Nation, or to impose its own policy choice on neighboring States. See *e.g., Healy* v. *Beer Institute,* 491 U. S. 324, 335–336. Accordingly, the economic penalties that a State inflicts on those who transgress its laws, whether the penalties are legislatively authorized fines or judicially imposed punitive damages, must be supported by the State's interest in protecting its own consumers and economy, rather than those of other States or the entire Nation. Gore's award must therefore be analyzed in the light of conduct that occurred solely within Alabama, with consideration being given only to the interests of Alabama consumers. Pp. 7–13.

(b) Elementary notions of fairness enshrined in this Court's constitutional jurisprudence dictate that a person receive fair notice not only of the conduct that will subject him to punishment but also of the severity of the penalty that a State may impose. Three guideposts, each of which indicates that BMW did not receive adequate notice of the magnitude of the sanction that Alabama might impose, lead to the conclusion that the $2 million award is grossly excessive. Pp. 13–14.

(c) None of the aggravating factors associated with the first (and perhaps most important) indicium of a punitive damages award's excessiveness—the degree of reprehensibility of the defendant's conduct, see *e.g., Day* v. *Woodworth,* 13 How. 363, 371—is present here. The harm BMW inflicted on Gore was purely economic; the presale repainting had no effect on the car's performance, safety features, or appearance; and BMW's conduct evinced no indifference to or reckless disregard for the health and safety of others. Gore's contention that BMW's nondisclosure was particularly reprehensible because it formed part of a nationwide pattern of tortious conduct is rejected, because a corporate executive could reasonably have interpreted the relevant state statutes as establishing safe harbors for nondisclosure of presumptively minor repairs, and because there is no evidence either that BMW acted in bad faith when it sought to establish the appropriate line between minor damage and damage requiring disclosure to purchasers, or that it persisted in its course of conduct after it had been adjudged unlawful. Finally, there is no evidence that BMW engaged in deliberate false statements, acts of affirmative misconduct, or concealment of evidence of improper motive. Pp. 14–20.

(d) The second (and perhaps most commonly cited) indicium of excessiveness—the ratio between the plaintiff's compensatory damages and the amount of the punitive damages, see *e.g., TXO,* 509 U. S., at 459—also weighs against Gore, because his $2 million award is 500 times the amount of his actual harm as determined by the jury, and there is no suggestion that he or any other BMW purchaser was threatened with any additional potential harm by BMW's nondisclosure policy. Although it is not possible to draw a mathematical bright line between the constitutionally acceptable and the constitutionally unacceptable that would fit every case, see, *e.g., id.,* at 458, the ratio here is clearly outside the acceptable range. Pp. 20–23.

(e) Gore's punitive damages award is not saved by the third relevant indicium of excessiveness—the difference between it and the civil or criminal sanctions that could be imposed for comparable misconduct, see, *e.g., Pacific Mut. Life Ins. Co.* v. *Haslip,* 499 U. S. 1, 23—because $2 million is substantially greater than Alabama's applicable $2,000 fine and the penalties imposed in other States for similar malfeasance, and because none of the pertinent statutes or interpretive decisions would have put an out-of-state distributor on notice that it might be subject to a multimillion dollar sanction. Moreover, in the absence of a BMW history of noncompliance with known statutory requirements, there is no basis for assuming that a more modest sanction would not have been sufficient. Pp. 23–25.

(f) Thus, BMW's conduct was not sufficiently egregious to justify the severe punitive sanction imposed against it. Whether the appropriate remedy requires a new trial or merely an independent determination by the Alabama Supreme Court of the award necessary to vindicate Alabama consumers' economic interests is a matter for that court to address in the first instance. Pp. 25–26.

646 So. 2d 619, reversed and remanded.

STEVENS, J., delivered the opinion of the Court, in which O'CONNOR, KENNEDY, SOUTER, and BREYER, JJ., joined. BREYER, J., filed a concurring opinion, in which O'CONNOR and SOUTER, JJ., joined. SCALIA, J., filed a dissenting opinion, in which THOMAS, J., joined. GINSBURG, J., filed a dissenting opinion, in which REHNQUIST, C. J., joined.

SUPREME COURT OF THE UNITED STATES

Syllabus

UNITED STATES *v.* ARMSTRONG, et al.

CERTIORARI TO THE UNITED STATES COURT OF APPEALS FOR THE NINTH CIRCUIT

No. 95–157. Argued February 26, 1996—Decided May 13, 1996

In response to their indictment on "crack" cocaine and other federal charges, respondents filed a motion for discovery or for dismissal, alleging that they were selected for prosecution because they are black. The District Court granted the motion over the Government's argument, among others, that there was no evidence or allegation that it had failed to prosecute nonblack defendants. When the Government indicated it would not comply with the discovery order, the court dismissed the case. The *en banc* Ninth Circuit affirmed, holding that the proof requirements for a selective-prosecution claim do not compel a defendant to demonstrate that the Government has failed to prosecute others who are similarly situated.

Held: For a defendant to be entitled to discovery on a claim that he was singled out for prosecution on the basis of his race, he must make a threshold showing that the Government declined to prosecute similarly situated suspects of other races. Pp. 4–14.

(a) Contrary to respondents' contention, Federal Rule of Criminal Procedure 16, which governs discovery in criminal cases, does not support the result reached by the Ninth Circuit in this case. Rule 16(a)(1)(C)—which, *inter alia,* requires the Government to permit discovery of documents that are "material to the preparation of the . . .

defense" or "intended for use by the government as evidence in chief"—applies only to the preparation of the "defense" against the Government's case in chief, not to the preparation of selective-prosecution claims. This reading creates a perceptible symmetry between the types of documents referred to in the Rule. Moreover, its correctness is established beyond peradventure by Rule 16(a)(2), which, as relevant here, exempts from discovery the work product of government attorneys and agents made in connection with the case's investigation. Respondents' construction of "defense" as including selective-prosecution claims is implausible: It creates the anomaly of a defendant's being able to examine all government work product under Rule 16(a)(1)(C), except that which is most pertinent, the work product in connection with his own case, under Rule 16(a)(2). Pp. 4–6.

(b) Under the equal protection component of the Fifth Amendment's Due Process Clause, the decision whether to prosecute may not be based on an arbitrary classification such as race or religion. *Oyler* v. *Boles,* 368 U. S. 448, 456. In order to prove a selective-prosecution claim, the claimant must demonstrate that the prosecutorial policy had a discriminatory effect and was motivated by a discriminatory purpose. *Ibid.* To establish a discriminatory effect in a race case, the claimant must show that similarly situated individuals of a different race were not prosecuted. *Ah Sin* v. *Wittman,* 198 U. S. 500. *Batson* v. *Kentucky,* 476 U. S. 79, and *Hunter* v. *Underwood,* 471 U. S. 222, distinguished. Although *Ah Sin* involved federal review of a state conviction, a similar rule applies where the power of a federal court is invoked to challenge an exercise of one of the core powers of the Executive Branch of the Federal Government, the power to prosecute. Discovery imposes many of the costs present when the Government must respond to a prima facie case of selective prosecution. Assuming that discovery is available on an appropriate showing in aid of a selective-prosecution claim, see *Wade* v. *United States,* 504 U. S. 181, the justifications for a rigorous standard of proof for the elements of such a case thus require a correspondingly rigorous standard for discovery in aid of it. Thus, in order to establish entitlement to such discovery, a defendant must produce credible evidence that similarly situated defendants of other races could have been prosecuted, but were not. In this case, respondents have not met this required threshold. Pp. 6–14.

48 F. 3d 1508, reversed and remanded.

REHNQUIST, C. J., delivered the opinion of the Court, in which O'CONNOR, SCALIA, KENNEDY, SOUTER, THOMAS, and GINSBURG, JJ., joined, and in which BREYER, J., joined in part. SOUTER, J., and GINSBURG, J., filed concurring opinions. BREYER, J., filed an opinion concurring in part and concurring in the judgment. STEVENS, J., filed a dissenting opinion.

SUPREME COURT OF THE UNITED STATES

Syllabus

BENNIS *v.* MICHIGAN

CERTIORARI TO THE SUPREME COURT OF MICHIGAN

No. 94–8729. Argued November 29, 1995—Decided March 4, 1996

Petitioner was a joint owner, with her husband, of an automobile in which her husband engaged in sexual activity with a prostitute. In declaring the automobile forfeit as a public nuisance under Michigan's statutory abatement scheme, the trial court permitted no offset for petitioner's interest, notwithstanding her lack of knowledge of her husband's activity. The Michigan Court of Appeals reversed, but was in turn reversed by the State Supreme Court, which concluded, *inter alia,* that Michigan's failure to provide an innocent-owner defense was without federal constitutional consequence under this Court's decisions.

Held: The forfeiture order did not offend the Due Process Clause of the Fourteenth Amendment or the Takings Clause of the Fifth Amendment. Pp. 4–12.

(a) Michigan's abatement scheme has not deprived petitioner of her interest in the forfeited car without due process. Her claim that she was entitled to contest the abatement by showing that she did not know that her husband would use the car to violate state law is defeated by a long and unbroken line of cases in which this Court has held that an owner's interest in property may be forfeited by reason of the use to which the property is put even though the owner did not know that it was to be put to such use. See, *e.g., Van Oster* v. *Kansas,* 272 U. S. 465, 467–468, and *Calero-Toledo* v. *Pearson Yacht Leasing Co.,* 416 U. S. 663, 668, 683; *Foucha* v. *Louisiana,* 504 U. S. 71, 80, and *Austin* v. *United States,* 509 U. S. ___, ___, distinguished. These cases are too firmly fixed in the country's punitive and remedial jurisprudence to be now displaced. Cf. *J. W. Goldsmith, Jr.-Grant Co.* v. *United States,* 254 U. S. 505, 511. Pp. 4–11.

(b) Michigan's abatement scheme has not taken petitioner's property for public use without compensation. Because the forfeiture proceeding did not violate the Fourteenth Amendment, her property in the automobile was transferred by virtue of that proceeding to the State. The government may not be required to compensate an owner for property which it has already lawfully acquired under the exercise of governmental authority other than the power of eminent domain. See, *e.g., United States* v. *Fuller,* 409 U. S. 488, 492. P. 11.

447 Mich. 719, 527 N. W. 2d 483, affirmed.

REHNQUIST, C. J., delivered the opinion of the Court, in which O'CONNOR, SCALIA, THOMAS, and GINSBURG, JJ., joined. THOMAS, J., and GINSBURG, J., filed concurring opinions. STEVENS, J., filed a dissenting opinion, in which SOUTER and BREYER, JJ., joined. KENNEDY, J., filed a dissenting opinion.

UPDATES: NEW FEDERAL LEGISLATION

THE PRISON LITIGATION REFORM ACT (1996)

While only about 2,000 petitions per year concerning inmate problems were being filed with the courts in 1961, by 1975 the number of filings had increased to around 17,000, and by 1995 prisoners filed 41,679 civil-rights lawsuits in federal courts nationwide.[1] Some inmate-originated suits seemed patently ludicrous, and became the subject of much media coverage in the mid-1990s.[2] One such suit involved Robert Procup, a Florida State Prison inmate serving time for the murder of his business partner. Procup repeatedly sued Florida prison officials—once because he got only one roll with his dinner; again because he once didn't get a luncheon salad; a third time because prison provided TV-dinners didn't come with a drink; and a fourth time because his cell had no television. Two other well-publicized cases involved an inmate who went to court asking to be allowed to exercise religious freedom by attending prison chapel services in the nude; and an inmate who, thinking he could become pregnant via homosexual relations, sued prison doctors who wouldn't provide him with birth control pills. An infamous example of seemingly frivolous inmate lawsuits was one brought by inmates claiming religious freedoms and demanding that members of the Church of the New Song, or CONS, be provided steak and Harvey's Bristol Cream every Friday in order to celebrate communion. The CONS suit stayed in various courts for ten years before being finally thrown out.[3]

The huge number of inmate-originated lawsuits created a backlog of cases in many federal courts and was targeted by the media and some citizen's groups as an unnecessary waste of taxpayer money. The National Association of Attorneys General, which supports efforts to restrict frivolous inmate lawsuits, estimates that lawsuits filed by prisoners cost states more than $81 million a year in legal fees alone.[4]

In 1996, in an effort to restrict inmate filings to worthwhile cases, Congress enacted the federal Prison Litigation Reform Act (PLRA).[5] The Act was signed into law by President Clinton in April of that year. It:

- Requires inmates to pay a $120 federal-court filing fee.

- Limits the award of attorneys' fees in successful lawsuits brought by inmates.

- Requires judges to screen all inmate complaints against the federal government and to immediately dismiss those deemed frivolous or without merit.

- Revokes the good-time credits earned by federal prisoners toward early release if they file a malicious lawsuit.

- Bars prisoners from suing the federal government for mental or emotional injury unless there was also an associated physical injury.

- Mandates that court orders affecting prison administration cannot go any further than necessary to correct a violation of a particular inmate's civil rights.

- Makes it possible for state officials to have court orders lifted after two years unless there is a new finding of a continuing violation of federally guaranteed civil rights.

- Mandates that any court order requiring the release of prisoners due to over-crowding be approved by a three-member court before it can become effective.

A number of states have filed suit under PLRA, seeking to wrest control of their prison systems back from federal authorities. Federal authority to oversee prisons in 40 states and in the District of Columbia had been ordered during the 1980s by federal courts as a result of overcrowding or poor administration by local officials. The first successful bid to end federal oversight of an entire state system came in 1996 when control of the South Carolina prison system reverted back to state authorities. The state had yielded to federal oversight in a 1985 agreement. Iowa and Wisconsin have also sought relief under PLRA, and, as of this writing, New York, Michigan, Illinois and Connecticut are considering whether to file challenges.

Opponents of PLRA fear that it might stifle the filing of meritorious suits by inmates facing real deprivations. "Although the act was advertised as an attack on frivolous litigation, it actually is an attack on litigation of great merit," says Elizabeth Alexander of the American Civil Liberties Union's national prison project.[6] Ira Robbins, an American University law professor, adds: "a lot of the changes that have to be made to bring prisons up to minimum levels of decency aren't going to occur." In passing the Prison Litigation Reform Act, Robbins is concerned that "Congress has focused on efficiency at the expense of fairness."[7] Prisoners' rights organizations have vowed to challenge the PLRA in court, and Elizabeth Alexander, Executive Director of the ACLU Foundation's Prison Project says, "We believe that the major provisions of the PLRA are unconstitutional and will be held so as a violation of the separation of powers and the due process clause of the Constitution." Ms. Alexander promised that the ACLU would "challenge PLRA in every court in which it comes up."[8] Excerpts from the law follow:

TITLE VIII—PRISON LITIGATION REFORM

SEC. 801. SHORT TITLE.

This title may be cited as the 'Prison Litigation Reform Act of 1995.'

SEC. 802. APPROPRIATE REMEDIES FOR PRISON CONDITIONS.

(a) IN GENERAL—Section 3626 of title 18, United States Code, is amended to read as follows:

"Sec. 3626. Appropriate remedies with respect to prison conditions

(a) REQUIREMENTS FOR RELIEF—

(1) PROSPECTIVE RELIEF—

(A) Prospective relief in any civil action with respect to prison conditions shall extend no further than necessary to correct the violation of the Federal right of a particular plaintiff or plaintiffs. The court shall not grant or approve any prospective relief unless the court finds that such relief is narrowly drawn, extends no further than necessary to correct the violation of the Federal right, and is the least intrusive means necessary to correct the violation of the Federal right. The court shall give substantial weight to any adverse impact on public safety or the operation of a criminal justice system caused by the relief.

(B) The court shall not order any prospective relief that requires or permits a government official to exceed his or her authority under State or local law or otherwise violates State or local law, unless—

(i) Federal law permits such relief to be ordered in violation of State or local law;

(ii) the relief is necessary to correct the violation of a Federal right; and

(iii) no other relief will correct the violation of the Federal right.

(C) Nothing in this section shall be construed to authorize the courts, in exercising their remedial powers, to order the construction of prisons or the raising of taxes, or to repeal or detract from otherwise applicable limitations on the remedial powers of the courts.

(2) PRELIMINARY INJUNCTIVE RELIEF—In any civil action with respect to prison conditions, to the extent otherwise authorized by law, the court may enter a temporary restraining order or an order for preliminary injunctive relief. Preliminary injunctive relief must be narrowly drawn, extend no further than necessary to correct the harm the court finds requires preliminary relief, and be the least intrusive means necessary to correct that harm. The court shall give substantial weight to any adverse impact on public safety or the operation of a criminal justice system caused by the preliminary relief and shall respect the principles of comity set out in paragraph (1)(B) in tailoring any preliminary relief.

Preliminary injunctive relief shall automatically expire on the date that is 90 days after its entry, unless the court makes the findings required under subsection (a)(1) for the entry of prospective relief and makes the order final before the expiration of the 90-day period.

(3) PRISONER RELEASE ORDER—

(A) In any civil action with respect to prison conditions, no prisoner release order shall be entered unless—

(i) a court has previously entered an order for less intrusive relief that has failed to remedy the deprivation of the Federal right sought to be remedied through the prisoner release order; and

(ii) the defendant has had a reasonable amount of time to comply with the previous court orders.

(B) In any civil action in Federal court with respect to prison conditions, a prisoner release order shall be entered only by a three-judge court in accordance with section 2284 of title 28, if the requirements of subparagraph (E) have been met.

(C) A party seeking a prisoner release order in Federal court shall file with any request for such relief, a request for a three-judge court and materials sufficient to demonstrate that the requirements of subparagraph (A) have been met.

(D) If the requirements under subparagraph (A) have been met, a Federal judge before whom a civil action with respect to prison conditions is pending who believes that a prison release order should be considered may *sua sponte* request the convening of a three-judge court to determine whether a prisoner release order should be entered.

(E) The three-judge court shall enter a prisoner release order only if the court finds by clear and convincing evidence that—

(i) crowding is the primary cause of the violation of a Federal right; and

(ii) no other relief will remedy the violation of the Federal right. (F) Any State or local official or unit of government whose jurisdiction or function includes the appropriation of funds for the construction, operation, or maintenance of program facilities, or the prosecution or custody of persons who may be released from, or not admitted to, a prison as a result of a prisoner release order shall have standing to oppose the imposition or continuation in effect of such relief and to seek termination of such relief, and shall have the right to intervene in any proceeding relating to such relief.

(b) TERMINATION OF RELIEF—

(1) TERMINATION OF PROSPECTIVE RELIEF—

(A) In any civil action with respect to prison conditions in which prospective relief is ordered, such relief shall be terminable upon the motion of any party or intervener—

(i) 2 years after the date the court granted or approved the prospective relief;

(ii) 1 year after the date the court has entered an order denying termination of prospective relief under this paragraph; or

(iii) in the case of an order issued on or before the date of enactment of the Prison Litigation Reform Act, 2 years after such date of enactment. (B) Nothing in this section shall prevent the parties from agreeing to terminate or modify relief before the relief is terminated under subparagraph (A). (2) IMMEDIATE TERMINATION OF PROSPECTIVE RELIEF—In any civil action with respect to prison conditions, a defendant or intervener shall be entitled to the immediate termination of any prospective relief if the relief was approved or granted in the absence of a finding by the court that the relief is narrowly drawn, extends no further than necessary to correct the violation of the Federal right, and is the least intrusive means necessary to correct the violation of the Federal right.

(3) LIMITATION—Prospective relief shall not terminate if the court makes written findings based on the record that prospective relief remains necessary to correct a current or ongoing violation of the Federal right, extends no further than necessary to cor-

rect the violation of the Federal right, and that the prospective relief is narrowly drawn and the least intrusive means to correct the violation.

(4) TERMINATION OR MODIFICATION OF RELIEF—Nothing in this section shall prevent any party or intervener from seeking modification or termination before the relief is terminable under paragraph (1) or (2), to the extent that modification or termination would otherwise be legally permissible. (c) SETTLEMENTS—

(1) CONSENT DECREES—In any civil action with respect to prison conditions, the court shall not enter or approve a consent decree unless it complies with the limitations on relief set forth in subsection (a)...

(1) IN GENERAL—

(A) In any civil action in a Federal court with respect to prison conditions, the court may appoint a special master who shall be disinterested and objective and who will give due regard to the public safety, to conduct hearings on the record and prepare proposed findings of fact.

(B) The court shall appoint a special master under this subsection during the remedial phase of the action only upon a finding that the remedial phase will be sufficiently complex to warrant the appointment.

(2) APPOINTMENT—

(A) If the court determines that the appointment of a special master is necessary, the court shall request that the defendant institution and the plaintiff each submit a list of not more than 5 persons to serve as a special master.

(B) Each party shall have the opportunity to remove up to 3 persons from the opposing party's list.

(C) The court shall select the master from the persons remaining on the list after the operation of subparagraph (B).

(3) INTERLOCUTORY APPEAL—Any party shall have the right to an interlocutory appeal of the judge's selection of the special master under this subsection, on the ground of partiality.

(4) COMPENSATION—The compensation to be allowed to a special master under this section shall be based on an hourly rate not greater than the hourly rate established under section 3006A for payment of court-appointed counsel, plus costs reasonably incurred by the special master. Such compensation and costs shall be paid with funds appropriated to the Judiciary.

(5) REGULAR REVIEW OF APPOINTMENT—In any civil action with respect to prison conditions in which a special master is appointed under this subsection, the court shall review the appointment of the special master every 6 months to determine whether the services of the special master continue to be required under paragraph (1). In no event shall the appointment of a special master extend beyond the termination of the relief.

(6) LIMITATIONS ON POWERS AND DUTIES—A special master appointed under this subsection—

(A) may be authorized by a court to conduct hearings and prepare proposed findings of fact, which shall be made on the record;

(B) shall not make any findings or communications exparte;

(C) may be authorized by a court to assist in the development of remedial plans; and

(D) may be removed at any time, but shall be relieved of the appointment upon the termination of relief. (g) DEFINITIONS—As used in this section—

(1) the term 'consent decree' means any relief entered by the court that is based in whole or in part upon the consent or acquiescence of the parties but does not include private settlements;

(2) the term 'civil action with respect to prison conditions' means any civil proceeding arising under Federal law with respect to the conditions of confinement or the effects of actions by government officials on the lives of persons confined in prison, but does not include *habeas corpus* proceedings challenging the fact or duration of confinement in prison;

(3) the term 'prisoner' means any person subject to incarceration, detention, or admission to any facility who is accused of, convicted of, sentenced for, or adjudicated delinquent for, violations of criminal law or the terms and conditions of parole, probation, pretrial release, or diversionary program;

(4) the term 'prisoner release order' includes any order, including a temporary restraining order or preliminary injunctive relief, that has the purpose or effect of reducing or limiting the prison population, or that directs the release from or nonadmission of prisoners to a prison;

(5) the term 'prison' means any Federal, State, or local facility that incarcerates or detains juveniles or adults accused of, convicted of, sentenced for, or adjudicated delinquent for, violations of criminal law;

(6) the term 'private settlement agreement' means an agreement entered into among the parties that is not subject to judicial enforcement other than the reinstatement of the civil proceeding that the agreement settled;

(7) the term 'prospective relief' means all relief other than compensatory monetary damages;

(8) the term 'special master' means any person appointed by a Federal court pursuant to Rule 53 of the Federal Rules of Civil Procedure or pursuant to any inherent power of the court to exercise the powers of a master, regardless of the title or description given by the court; and

(9) the term 'relief' means all relief in any form that may be granted or approved by the court, and includes consent decrees but does not include private settlement agreements." ...

(d) SUITS BY PRISONERS—Section 7 of the Act (42 U.S.C. 1997e) is amended to read as follows:

"SEC. 7. SUITS BY PRISONERS.

(a) APPLICABILITY OF ADMINISTRATIVE REMEDIES—No action shall be brought with respect to prison conditions under section 1979 of the Revised Statutes of the United States (42 U.S.C. 1983), or any other Federal law, by a prisoner confined in any jail, prison, or other correctional facility until such administrative remedies as are available are exhausted.

(b) FAILURE OF STATE TO ADOPT OR ADHERE TO ADMINISTRATIVE GRIEVANCE PROCEDURE—The failure of a State to adopt or adhere to an administrative grievance procedure shall not constitute the basis for an action under section 3 or 5 of this Act.

(c) DISMISSAL—

(1) The court shall on its own motion or on the motion of a party dismiss any action brought with respect to prison conditions under section 1979 of the Revised Statutes of the United States (42 U.S.C. 1983), or any other Federal law, by a prisoner confined in any jail, prison, or other correctional facility if the court is satisfied that the action is frivolous, malicious, fails to state a claim upon which relief can be granted, or seeks monetary relief from a defendant who is immune from such relief.

(2) In the event that a claim is, on its face, frivolous, malicious, fails to state a claim upon which relief can be granted, or seeks monetary relief from a defendant who is immune from such relief, the court may dismiss the underlying claim without first requiring the exhaustion of administrative remedies.

(d) ATTORNEY'S FEES—(1) In any action brought by a prisoner who is confined to any jail, prison, or other correctional facility, in which attorney's fees are authorized under section 2 of the Revised Statutes of the United States (42 U.S.C. 1988), such fees shall not be awarded, except to the extent that—(A) the fee was directly and reasonably incurred in proving an actual violation of the plaintiff's rights protected by a statute pursuant to which a fee may be awarded under section 2 of the Revised Statutes; and (B) (i) the amount of the fee is proportionately related to the court ordered relief for the violation; or (ii) the fee was directly and reasonably incurred in enforcing the relief ordered for the violation. (2) Whenever a monetary judgment is awarded in an action described in paragraph (1), a portion of the judgment (not to exceed 25 percent) shall be applied to satisfy the amount of attorney's fees awarded against the defendant. If the award of attorney's fees is not greater than 150 percent of the judgment, the excess shall be paid by the defendant.

(3) No award of attorney's fees in an action described in paragraph (1) shall be based on an hourly rate greater than 150 percent of the hourly rate established under section 3006A of title 18, United States Code, for payment of court-appointed counsel.

(4) Nothing in this subsection shall prohibit a prisoner from entering into an agreement to pay an attorney's fee in an amount greater than the amount authorized under this subsection, if the fee is paid by the individual rather than by the defendant pursuant to section 2 of the Revised Statutes of the United States (42 U.S.C. 1988). (e) LIMITATION ON RECOVERY—No Federal civil action may be brought by a prisoner confined in a jail, prison, or other correctional facility, for mental or emotional injury suffered while in custody without a prior showing of physical injury.

(f) HEARINGS—

(1) To the extent practicable, in any action brought with respect to prison conditions in Federal court pursuant to section 1979 of the Revised Statutes of the United States (42 U.S.C. 1983), or any other Federal law, by a prisoner confined in any jail, prison, or other correctional facility, pretrial proceedings in which the prisoner's participation is required or permitted shall be conducted by telephone, video conference, or other telecommunications technology without removing the prisoner from the facility in which the prisoner is confined.

(2) Subject to the agreement of the official of the Federal, State, or local unit of government with custody over the prisoner, hearings may be conducted at the facility in which the prisoner is confined. To the extent practicable, the court shall allow counsel to participate by telephone, video conference, or other communications technology in any hearing held at the facility....

SEC. 804. PROCEEDINGS IN *FORMA PAUPERIS.*

(a) FILING FEES—Section 1915 of title 28, United States Code, is amended—

(1) in subsection (a)—

(A) by striking '(a) Any' and inserting (B) by striking 'and costs';

(C) by striking 'makes affidavit' and inserting 'submits an affidavit that includes a statement of all assets such prisoner possesses';

(D) by striking 'such costs' and inserting 'such fees';

(E) by striking 'he' each place it appears and inserting 'the person';

(F) by adding immediately after paragraph (1), the following new paragraph:

(2) A prisoner seeking to bring a civil action or appeal a judgment in a civil action or proceeding without prepayment of fees or security therefor, in addition to filing the affidavit filed under paragraph (1), shall submit a certified copy of the trust fund account

statement (or institutional equivalent) for the prisoner for the 6-month period immediately preceding the filing of the complaint or notice of appeal, obtained from the appropriate official of each prison at which the prisoner is or was confined.'; and (G) by striking 'An appeal' and inserting '(3) An appeal'; (2) by redesignating subsections (b), (c), (d), and (e) as subsections (c), (d), (e), and (f), respectively;

(3) by inserting after subsection (a) the following new subsection: "(B)

(1) Notwithstanding subsection (a), if a prisoner brings a civil action or files an appeal in *forma pauperis,* the prisoner shall be required to pay the full amount of a filing fee. The court shall assess and, when funds exist, collect, as a partial payment of any court fees required by law, an initial partial filing fee of 20 percent of the greater of—

(A) the average monthly deposits to the prisoner's account; or

(B) the average monthly balance in the prisoner's account for the 6-month period immediately preceding the filing of the complaint or notice of appeal. (2) After payment of the initial partial filing fee, the prisoner shall be required to make monthly payments of 20 percent of the preceding month's income credited to the prisoner's account. The agency having custody of the prisoner shall forward payments from the prisoner's account to the clerk of the court each time the amount in the account exceeds $10 until the filing fees are paid.

(3) In no event shall the filing fee collected exceed the amount of fees permitted by statute for the commencement of a civil action or an appeal of a civil action or criminal judgment.

(4) In no event shall a prisoner be prohibited from bringing a civil action or appealing a civil or criminal judgment for the reason that the prisoner has no assets and no means by which to pay the initial partial filing fee."; (4) in subsection (c), as redesignated by paragraph (2), by striking 'subsection (a) of this section' and inserting 'subsections (a) and (b) and the prepayment of any partial filing fee as may be required under subsection (b)'; and

(5) by amending subsection (e), as redesignated by paragraph (2), to read as follows: "(e)

(1) The court may request an attorney to represent any person unable to afford counsel.

(2) Notwithstanding any filing fee, or any portion thereof, that may have been paid, the court shall dismiss the case at any time if the court determines that—

(A) the allegation of poverty is untrue; or

(B) the action or appeal—

(i) is frivolous or malicious;

(ii) fails to state a claim on which relief may be granted; or

(iii) seeks monetary relief against a defendant who is immune from such relief...

(d) SUCCESSIVE CLAIMS—Section 1915 of title 28, United States Code, is amended by adding at the end the following new subsection:

"(g) In no event shall a prisoner bring a civil action or appeal a judgment in a civil action or proceeding under this section if the prisoner has, on 3 or more prior occasions, while incarcerated or detained in any facility, brought an action or appeal in a court of the United States that was dismissed on the grounds that it is frivolous, malicious, or fails to state a claim upon which relief may be granted, unless the prisoner is under imminent danger of serious physical injury."

(e) DEFINITION—Section 1915 of title 28, United States Code, is amended by adding at the end the following new subsection:

"(h) As used in this section, the term 'prisoner' means any person incarcerated or detained in any facility who is accused of, convicted of, sentenced for, or adjudicated delinquent for, violations of criminal law or the terms and conditions of parole, probation, pretrial release, or diversionary program."

SEC. 805. JUDICIAL SCREENING.

(a) IN GENERAL—Chapter 123 of title 28, United States Code, is amended by inserting after section 1915 the following new section: "Sec. 1915A. Screening."

(a) SCREENING—The court shall review, before docketing, if feasible or, in any event, as soon as practicable after docketing, a complaint in a civil action in which a prisoner seeks redress from a governmental entity or officer or employee of a governmental entity.

(b) GROUNDS FOR DISMISSAL—On review, the court shall identify cognizable claims or dismiss the complaint, or any portion of the complaint, if the complaint —

(1) is frivolous, malicious, or fails to state a claim upon which relief may be granted; or

(2) seeks monetary relief from a defendant who is immune from such relief. (c) DEFINITION—As used in this section, the term 'prisoner' means any person incarcerated or detained in any facility who is accused of, convicted of, sentenced for, or adjudicated delinquent for, violations of criminal law or the terms and conditions of parole, probation, pretrial release, or diversionary program…"

SEC. 806. FEDERAL TORT CLAIMS.

Section 1346(b) of title 28, United States Code, is amended—

(1) by striking '(b)' and inserting '(b)(1)'; and

(2) by adding at the end the following:

(2) No person convicted of a felony who is incarcerated while awaiting sentencing or while serving a sentence may bring a civil action against the United States or an agency, officer, or employee of the Government, for mental or emotional injury suffered while in custody without a prior showing of physical injury.

SEC. 807. PAYMENT OF DAMAGE AWARD IN SATISFACTION OF PENDING RESTITUTION ORDERS.

Any compensatory damages awarded to a prisoner in connection with a civil action brought against any Federal, State, or local jail, prison, or correctional facility or against any official or agent of such jail, prison, or correctional facility, shall be paid directly to satisfy any outstanding restitution orders pending against the prisoner. The remainder of any such award after full payment of all pending restitution orders shall be forwarded to the prisoner.

SEC. 808. NOTICE TO CRIME VICTIMS OF PENDING DAMAGE AWARD.

Prior to payment of any compensatory damages awarded to a prisoner in connection with a civil action brought against any Federal, State, or local jail, prison, or correctional facility or against any official or agent of such jail, prison, or correctional facility, reasonable efforts shall be made to notify the victims of the crime for which the prisoner was convicted and incarcerated concerning the pending payment of any such compensatory damages.

SEC. 809. EARNED RELEASE CREDIT OR GOOD TIME CREDIT REVOCATION.

(a) IN GENERAL—Chapter 123 of title 28, United States Code, is amended by adding at the end the following new section:

Sec. 1932. Revocation of earned release credit.

In any civil action brought by an adult convicted of a crime and confined in a Federal correctional facility, the court may order the revocation of such earned good time credit under section 3624(b) of title 18, United States Code, that has not yet vested, if, on its own motion or the motion of any party, the court finds that—

(1) the claim was filed for a malicious purpose;

(2) the claim was filed solely to harass the party against which it was filed; or

(3) the claimant testifies falsely or otherwise knowingly presents false evidence or information to the court.

SEC. 810. SEVERABILITY.

If any provision of this title, an amendment made by this title, or the application of such provision or amendment to any person or circumstance is held to be unconstitutional, the remainder of this title, the amendments made by this title, and the application of the provisions of such to any person or circumstance shall not be affected thereby.

COMMUNICATIONS DECENCY ACT OF 1996

In 1996, amidst fierce debate, the U.S. Congress passed, and President Clinton signed, a law intended to control the availability of obscene materials on the Internet. Entitled the Communications Decency Act (CDA), the new law was part of the Telecommunications Act of 1996. The CDA makes it a federal offense for anyone to distribute "indecent" or "patently offensive" material to minors over computer networks such as the Internet or commercial on-line services. The law provides for prison terms of up to two years and a $250,000 fine if indecent material is transmitted to minors.

Opponents of the law claim that it unconstitutionally restricts free speech because it is not technologically possible for providers of access or content on the Internet to prevent minors from obtaining indecent materials intended for adults. "The senders . . . have no ability to ensure that their messages are only available to adults," says Harvard University computer consultant Scott Bradner.[9] "It is also not possible for an Internet service provider . . . to screen out all or even most content that could be deemed 'indecent' or 'patently offensive,'" added Bradner.

In mid-1996 a three-judge federal district court agreed with opponents of the CDA and issued a preliminary injunction barring enforcement of portions of the act. The unanimous decision held that speech over the Internet should be given the broadest possible constitutional protections—much like that now accorded to newspapers and magazines—as opposed to tighter restrictions on broacast media such as television. "As the most participatory form of mass speech yet developed, the Internet deserves the highest protection from governmental intrusion," said U.S. District Judge Stewart Dalzell, a member of the judicial panel.[10] "Just as the strength of [the] Internet is chaos, so the strength of our liberty depends upon the chaos and cacophony of the unfettered speech the First Amendment protects," Dalzell wrote.

The ultimate fate of the CDA will undoubtedly be decided by the U.S. Supreme Court which, as this supplement is being printed, is hearing an appeal of the district court's 1996 verdict. The case before the Court, *Reno* v. *ACLU,* has been described as "one of the most important free-speech cases of the century." Due to weaknesses in the law already convincingly identified by ACLU attorneys, both sides in the case now expect that the CDA will be rewritten during the coming congressional term. Excerpts from the current version of the CDA follow.

SUBTITLE A—OBSCENE, HARASSING, AND WRONGFUL UTILIZATION OF TELECOMMUNICATIONS FACILITIES

SEC. 501. SHORT TITLE.

This title may be cited as the 'Communications Decency Act of 1996.'

SEC. 502. OBSCENE OR HARASSING USE OF TELECOMMUNICATIONS FACILITIES UNDER THE COMMUNICATIONS ACT OF 1934.

Section 223 (47 U.S.C. 223) is amended—

(1) by striking subsection (a) and inserting in lieu thereof:

'(a) Whoever—

'(1) in interstate or foreign communications—

'(A) by means of a telecommunications device knowingly—

'(i) makes, creates, or solicits, and

'(ii) initiates the transmission of, any comment, request, suggestion, proposal, image, or other communication which is obscene, lewd, lascivious, filthy or indecent, with intent to annoy, abuse, threaten, or harass another person;

'(B) by means of a telecommunications device knowingly—

'(i) makes, creates, or solicits, and

'(ii) initiates the transmission of, any comment, request, suggestion, proposal, image, or other communication which is obscene or indecent, knowing that the recipient of the communication is under 18 years of age, regardless of whether the maker of such communication placed the call or initiated the communication;

'(C) makes a telephone call or utilizes a telecommunications device, whether or not conversation or communication ensues, without disclosing his identity and with intent to annoy, abuse, threaten, or harass any person at the called number or who receives the communications;

'(D) makes or causes the telephone of another repeatedly or continuously to ring, with intent to harass any person at the called number; or

'(E) makes repeated telephone calls or repeatedly initiates communication with a telecommunications device, during which conversation or communication ensues, solely to harass any person at the called number or who receives the communication; or

'(2) knowingly permits any telecommunications facility under his control to be used for any activity prohibited by paragraph (1) with the intent that it be used for such activity, shall be fined under title 18, United States Code, or imprisoned not more than two years, or both.;' and

(2) by adding at the end the following new subsections:

'(d) Whoever—

'(1) in interstate or foreign communications knowingly—

'(A) uses an interactive computer service to send to a specific person or persons under 18 years of age, or

'(B) uses any interactive computer service to display in a manner available to a person under 18 years of age, any comment, request, suggestion, proposal, image, or other communication that, in context, depicts or describes, in terms patently offensive as measured by contemporary community standards, sexual or excretory activities or organs, regardless of whether the user of such service placed the call or initiated the communication; or

'(2) knowingly permits any telecommunications facility under such person's control to be used for an activity prohibited by paragraph (1) with the intent that it be used for such activity, shall be fined under title 18, United States Code, or imprisoned not more than two years, or both.

'(e) In addition to any other defenses available by law:

'(1) No person shall be held to have violated subsection (a) or (d) solely for providing access or connection to or from a facility, system, or network not under that person's control, including transmission, downloading, intermediate storage, access software, or other related capabilities that are incidental to providing such access or connection that does not include the creation of the content of the communication.

'(2) The defenses provided by paragraph (1) of this subsection shall not be applicable to a person who is a conspirator with an entity actively involved in the creation or knowing distribution of communications that violate this section, or who knowingly advertises the availability of such communications.

'(3) The defenses provided in paragraph (1) of this subsection shall not be applicable to a person who provides access or connection to a facility, system, or network engaged in the violation of this section that is owned or controlled by such person.

'(4) No employer shall be held liable under this section for the actions of an employee or agent unless the employee's or agent's conduct is within the scope of his or her employment or agency and the employer (A) having knowledge of such conduct, authorizes or ratifies such conduct, or (B) recklessly disregards such conduct.

'(5) It is a defense to a prosecution under subsection (a)(1)(B) or (d), or under subsection (a)(2) with respect to the use of a facility for an activity under subsection (a)(1)(B) that a person—

'(A) has taken, in good faith, reasonable, effective, and appropriate actions under the circumstances to restrict or prevent access by minors to a communication specified in such subsections, which may involve any appropriate measures to restrict minors from such communications, including any method which is feasible under available technology; or

'(B) has restricted access to such communication by requiring use of a verified credit card, debit account, adult access code, or adult personal identification number.

'(6) The Commission may describe measures which are reasonable, effective, and appropriate to restrict access to prohibited communications under subsection (d). Nothing in this section authorizes the Commission to enforce, or is intended to provide the Commission with the authority to approve, sanction, or permit, the use of such measures. The Commission shall have no enforcement authority over the failure to utilize such measures. The Commission shall not endorse specific products relating to such measures. The use of such measures shall be admitted as evidence of good faith efforts for purposes of paragraph (5) in any action arising under subsection (d). Nothing in this section shall be construed to treat interactive computer services as common carriers or telecommunications carriers.

'(f)(1) No cause of action may be brought in any court or administrative agency against any person on account of any activity that is not in violation of any law punishable by criminal or civil penalty, and that the person has taken in good faith to implement a defense authorized under this section or otherwise to restrict or prevent the transmission of, or access to, a communication specified in this section.

'(2) No State or local government may impose any liability for commercial activities or actions by commercial entities, nonprofit libraries, or institutions of higher education in connection with an activity or action described in subsection (a)(2) or (d) that is inconsistent with the treatment of those activities or actions under this section: *Provided, however,* That nothing herein shall preclude any State or local government from enacting and enforcing complementary oversight, liability, and regulatory systems, procedures, and requirements, so long as such systems, procedures, and requirements govern only intrastate services and do not result in the imposition of inconsistent rights, duties or obligations on the provision of interstate services. Nothing in this subsection shall preclude any State or local government from governing conduct not covered by this section.

'(g) Nothing in subsection (a), (d), (e), or (f) or in the defenses to prosecution under subsection (a) or (d) shall be construed to affect or limit the application or enforcement of any other Federal law.

'(h) For purposes of this section—

'(1) The use of the term 'telecommunications device' in this section—

'(A) shall not impose new obligations on broadcasting station licensees and cable operators covered by obscenity and indecency provisions elsewhere in this Act; and

'(B) does not include an interactive computer service.

'(2) The term 'interactive computer service' has the meaning provided in section 230(e)(2).

'(3) The term 'access software' means software (including client or server software) or enabling tools that do not create or provide the content of the communication but that allow a user to do any one or more of the following:

'(A) filter, screen, allow, or disallow content;

'(B) pick, choose, analyze, or digest content; or

'(C) transmit, receive, display, forward, cache, search,

subset, organize, reorganize, or translate content.

'(4) The term 'institution of higher education' has the meaning provided in section 1201 of the Higher Education Act of 1965 (20 U.S.C. 1141).

'(5) The term 'library' means a library eligible for participation in State-based plans for funds under title III of the Library Services and Construction Act (20 U.S.C. 355e et seq.).'...

SEC. 509. ONLINE FAMILY EMPOWERMENT.

Title II of the Communications Act of 1934 (47 U.S.C. 201 et seq.) is amended by adding at the end the following new section:

'SEC. 230. PROTECTION FOR PRIVATE BLOCKING AND SCREENING OF OFFENSIVE MATERIAL.

'(a) FINDINGS—The Congress finds the following:

'(1) The rapidly developing array of Internet and other interactive computer services available to individual Americans represent an extraordinary advance in the availability of educational and informational resources to our citizens.

'(2) These services offer users a great degree of control over the information that they receive, as well as the potential for even greater control in the future as technology develops.

'(3) The Internet and other interactive computer services offer a forum for a true diversity of political discourse, unique opportunities for cultural development, and myriad avenues for intellectual activity.

'(4) The Internet and other interactive computer services have flourished, to the benefit of all Americans, with a minimum of government regulation.

'(5) Increasingly Americans are relying on interactive media for a variety of political, educational, cultural, and entertainment services.

'(b) POLICY- It is the policy of the United States—

'(1) to promote the continued development of the Internet and other interactive computer services and other interactive media;

'(2) to preserve the vibrant and competitive free market that presently exists for the Internet and other interactive computer services, unfettered by Federal or State regulation;

'(3) to encourage the development of technologies which maximize user control over what information is received by individuals, families, and schools who use the Internet and other interactive computer services;

'(4) to remove disincentives for the development and utilization of blocking and filtering technologies that empower parents to restrict their children's access to objectionable or inappropriate online material; and

'(5) to ensure vigorous enforcement of Federal criminal laws to deter and punish trafficking in obscenity, stalking, and harassment by means of computer.

'(c) PROTECTION FOR 'GOOD SAMARITAN' BLOCKING AND SCREENING OF OFFENSIVE MATERIAL—

'(1) TREATMENT OF PUBLISHER OR SPEAKER—No provider or user of an interactive computer service shall be treated as the publisher or speaker of any information provided by another information content provider.

'(2) CIVIL LIABILITY-—No provider or user of an interactive computer service shall be held liable on account of—

'(A) any action voluntarily taken in good faith to restrict access to or availability of material that the provider or user considers to be obscene, lewd, lascivious, filthy, excessively violent, harassing, or otherwise objectionable, whether or not such material is constitutionally protected; or

'(B) any action taken to enable or make available to information content providers or others the technical means to restrict access to material described in paragraph (1).

'(d) EFFECT ON OTHER LAWS—

'(1) NO EFFECT ON CRIMINAL LAW—Nothing in this section shall be construed to impair the enforcement of section 223 of this Act, chapter 71 (relating to obscenity) or 110 (relating to sexual exploitation of children) of title 18, United States Code, or any other Federal criminal statute.

'(2) NO EFFECT ON INTELLECTUAL PROPERTY LAW—Nothing in this section shall be construed to limit or expand any law pertaining to intellectual property.

'(3) STATE LAW—Nothing in this section shall be construed to prevent any State from enforcing any State law that is consistent with this section. No cause of action may be brought and no liability may be imposed under any State or local law that is inconsistent with this section.

'(4) NO EFFECT ON COMMUNICATIONS PRIVACY LAW—Nothing in this section shall be construed to limit the application of the Electronic Communications Privacy Act of 1986 or any of the amendments made by such Act, or any similar State law.

'(e) DEFINITIONS-—As used in this section:

'(1) INTERNET—The term 'Internet' means the international computer network of both Federal and non-Federal interoperable packet switched data networks.

'(2) INTERACTIVE COMPUTER SERVICE—The term 'interactive computer service' means any information service, system, or access software provider that provides or enables computer access by multiple users to a computer server, including specifically a service or system that provides access to the Internet and such systems operated or services offered by libraries or educational institutions.

'(3) INFORMATION CONTENT PROVIDER—The term 'information content provider' means any person or entity that is responsible, in whole or in part, for the creation or development of information provided through the Internet or any other interactive computer service.

'(4) ACCESS SOFTWARE PROVIDER—The term 'access software provider' means a provider of software (including client or server software), or enabling tools that do any one or more of the following:

'(A) filter, screen, allow, or disallow content;

'(B) pick, choose, analyze, or digest content; or

'(C) transmit, receive, display, forward, cache, search, subset, organize, reorganize, or translate content.'.

SUBTITLE B—VIOLENCE

SEC. 551. PARENTAL CHOICE IN TELEVISION PROGRAMMING.

(a) FINDINGS—The Congress makes the following findings:

(1) Television influences children's perception of the values and behavior that are common and acceptable in society.

(2) Television station operators, cable television system operators, and video programmers should follow practices in connection with video programming that take into consideration that television broadcast and cable programming has established a uniquely pervasive presence in the lives of American children.

(3) The average American child is exposed to 25 hours of television each week and some children are exposed to as much as 11 hours of television a day.

(4) Studies have shown that children exposed to violent video programming at a young age have a higher tendency for violent and aggressive behavior later in life than children not so exposed, and that children exposed to violent video programming are prone to assume that acts of violence are acceptable behavior.

(5) Children in the United States are, on average, exposed to an estimated 8,000 murders and 100,000 acts of violence on television by the time the child completes elementary school.

(6) Studies indicate that children are affected by the pervasiveness and casual treatment of sexual material on television, eroding the ability of parents to develop responsible attitudes and behavior in their children.

(7) Parents express grave concern over violent and sexual video programming and strongly support technology that would give them greater control to block video programming in the home that they consider harmful to their children.

(8) There is a compelling governmental interest in empowering parents to limit the negative influences of video programming that is harmful to children.

(9) Providing parents with timely information about the nature of upcoming video programming and with the technological tools that allow them easily to block violent, sexual, or other programming that they believe harmful to their children is a nonintrusive and narrowly tailored means of achieving that compelling governmental interest.

(b) ESTABLISHMENT OF TELEVISION RATING CODE—

(1) AMENDMENT—Section 303 (47 U.S.C. 303) is amended by adding at the end the following:

'(w) Prescribe—

'(1) on the basis of recommendations from an advisory committee established by the Commission in accordance with section 551(b)(2) of the Telecommunications Act of 1996, guidelines and recommended procedures for the identification and rating of video programming that contains sexual, violent, or other indecent material about which parents should be informed before it is displayed to children: *Provided,* that nothing in this paragraph shall be construed to authorize any rating of video programming on the basis of its political or religious content; and

'(2) with respect to any video programming that has been rated, and in consultation with the television industry, rules requiring distributors of such video programming to transmit such rating to permit parents to block the display of video programming that they have determined is inappropriate for their children.'.

(2) ADVISORY COMMITTEE REQUIREMENTS—In establishing an advisory committee for purposes of the amendment made by paragraph (1) of this subsection, the Commission shall—

(A) ensure that such committee is composed of parents, television broadcasters, television programming producers, cable operators, appropriate public interest groups, and other interested individuals from the private sector and is fairly balanced in terms of political affiliation, the points of view represented, and the functions to be performed by the committee;

(B) provide to the committee such staff and resources as may be necessary to permit it to perform its functions efficiently and promptly; and

(C) require the committee to submit a final report of its recommendations within one year after the date of the appointment of the initial members.

(c) REQUIREMENT FOR MANUFACTURE OF TELEVISIONS THAT BLOCK PROGRAMS—Section 303 (47 U.S.C. 303), as amended by subsection (a), is further amended by adding at the end the following:

'(x) Require, in the case of an apparatus designed to receive television signals that are shipped in interstate commerce or manufactured in the United States and that have a picture screen 13 inches or greater in size (measured diagonally), that such apparatus be equipped with a feature designed to enable viewers to block display of all programs with a common rating, except as otherwise permitted by regulations pursuant to section 330(c)(4).'.

(d) SHIPPING OF TELEVISIONS THAT BLOCK PROGRAMS—

(1) REGULATIONS—Section 330 (47 U.S.C. 330) is amended—

(A) by redesignating subsection (c) as subsection (d); and

(B) by adding after subsection (b) the following new subsection (c):

'(c)(1) Except as provided in paragraph (2), no person shall ship in interstate commerce or manufacture in the United States any apparatus described in section 303(x) of this Act except in accordance with rules prescribed by the Commission pursuant to the authority granted by that section.

'(2) This subsection shall not apply to carriers transporting apparatus referred to in paragraph (1) without trading in it.

'(3) The rules prescribed by the Commission under this subsection shall provide for the oversight by the Commission of the adoption of standards by industry for blocking technology. Such rules shall require that all such apparatus be able to receive the rating signals which have been transmitted by way of line 21 of the vertical blanking interval and which conform to the signal and blocking specifications established by industry under the supervision of the Commission.

'(4) As new video technology is developed, the Commission shall take such action as the Commission determines appropriate to ensure that blocking service continues to be available to consumers. If the Commission determines that an alternative blocking technology exists that—

'(A) enables parents to block programming based on identifying programs without ratings,

'(B) is available to consumers at a cost which is comparable to the cost of technology that allows parents to block programming based on common ratings, and

'(C) will allow parents to block a broad range of programs on a multichannel system as effectively and as easily as technology that allows parents to block programming based on common ratings, the Commission shall amend the rules prescribed pursuant to section 303(x) to require that the apparatus described in such section be equipped with either the blocking technology described in such section or the alternative blocking technology described in this paragraph.'.

(2) CONFORMING AMENDMENT—Section 330(d), as redesignated by subsection (d)(1)(A), is amended by striking 'section 303(s), and section 303(u)' and inserting in lieu thereof 'and sections

303(s), 303(u), and 303(x)'.

(e) APPLICABILITY AND EFFECTIVE DATES—

(1) APPLICABILITY OF RATING PROVISION—The amendment made by subsection (b) of this section shall take effect 1 year after the date of enactment of this Act, but only if the Commission determines, in consultation with appropriate public interest groups and interested individuals from the private sector, that distributors of video programming have not, by such date—

(A) established voluntary rules for rating video programming that contains sexual, violent, or other indecent material about which parents should be informed before it is displayed to children, and such rules are acceptable to the Commission; and

(B) agreed voluntarily to broadcast signals that contain ratings of such programming.

(2) EFFECTIVE DATE OF MANUFACTURING PROVISION—In prescribing regulations to implement the amendment made by subsection (c), the Federal Communications Commission shall, after consultation with the television manufacturing industry, specify the effective date for the applicability of the requirement to the apparatus covered by such amendment, which date shall not be less than two years after the date of enactment of this Act.

SEC. 552. TECHNOLOGY FUND.

It is the policy of the United States to encourage broadcast television, cable, satellite, syndication, other video programming distributors, and relevant related industries (in consultation with appropriate public interest groups and interested individuals from the private sector) to—

(1) establish a technology fund to encourage television and electronics equipment manufacturers to facilitate the development of technology which would empower parents to block programming they deem inappropriate for their children and to encourage the availability thereof to low income parents;

(2) report to the viewing public on the status of the development of affordable, easy to use blocking technology; and

(3) establish and promote effective procedures, standards, systems, advisories, or other mechanisms for ensuring that users have easy and complete access to the information necessary to effectively utilize blocking technology and to encourage the availability thereof to low income parents.

SUBTITLE C—JUDICIAL REVIEW

SEC. 561. EXPEDITED REVIEW.

(a) THREE-JUDGE DISTRICT COURT HEARING—Notwithstanding any other provision of law, any civil action challenging the constitutionality, on its face, of this title or any amendment made by this title, or any provision thereof, shall be heard by a district court of 3 judges convened pursuant to the provisions of section 2284 of title 28, United States Code.

(b) APPELLATE REVIEW—Notwithstanding any other provision of law, an interlocutory or final judgment, decree, or order of the court of 3 judges in an action under subsection (a) holding this title or an amendment made by this title, or any provision thereof, unconstitutional shall be reviewable as a matter of right by direct appeal to the Supreme Court. Any such appeal shall be filed not more than 20 days after entry of such judgment, decree, or order.

THE "SHERMAN REPORT"—PREVENTING CRIME: WHAT WORKS, WHAT DOESN'T, WHAT'S PROMISING

In mid-1997 the "Sherman Report" was submitted to the U.S. Congress. Called "The most comprehensive study ever of crime prevention" by the New York Times, it had been commissioned years earlier by congressional investigators eager to learn whether the $3 billion dollars spent annually on crime prevention programs by the federal government were being spent effectively. The report was prepared by Lawrence W. Sherman, Denise Gottfredson, Doris MacKenzie, John Eck, Peter Reuter, Shawn Bushway, and others.

Researchers found that some of the most popular crime prevention programs, including boot camps, midnight basketball, neighborhood watches and drug education classes in schools, have little impact on crime. Researchers also questioned the effectiveness of the huge prison construction program undertaken throughout the nation during the past two decades. The study, however, did find promising results from some programs, particularly intensified police patrols in high-crime areas, drug treatment in prisons and home visits by nurses, social workers and others for infants in troubled families.

Most significantly, the study found that it remains difficult to assess federal crime-prevention programs because there is little rigorous, scientific evaluation of them. What follows are excerpts from the report's "Overview," written by Lawrence W. Sherman. The entire study can be accessed via the World Wide Web at http://www.ncjrs.org.

OVERVIEW

Mandate. In 1996 Congress required the Attorney General to provide a "comprehensive evaluation of the effectiveness" of over $3 Billion annually in Department of Justice grants to assist State and local law enforcement and communities in preventing crime. Congress required that the research for the evaluation be "independent in nature," and "employ rigorous and scientifically recognized standards and methodologies." It also called for the evaluation to give special emphasis to "factors that relate to juvenile crime and the effect of these programs on youth violence," including "risk factors in the community, schools, and family environments that contribute to juvenile violence." The Assistant Attorney General for the Office of Justice Programs asked the National Institute of Justice to commission an independent review of the relevant scientific literature, which exceeds 500 program impact evaluations.

PRIMARY CONCLUSION. This Report found that some prevention programs work, some do not, some are promising, and some have not been tested adequately. Given the evidence of promising and effective programs, the Report finds that **the effectiveness of Department of Justice funding depends heavily on whether it is directed to the urban neighborhoods where youth violence is highly concentrated.** Substantial reductions in national rates of serious crime can only be achieved by prevention in areas of concentrated poverty, where the majority of all homicides in the nation occur, and where homicide rates are 20 times the national average.

Primary Recommendation. Because the specific methods for preventing crime in areas of concentrated poverty are not well-developed and tested, the Congress can make most effective use of DOJ local assistance funding by providing better guidance about what works. A much larger part of the national crime prevention portfolio must be invested in rigorous testing of innovative programs, in order to identify the active ingredients of locally successful programs that can be recommended for adoption in similar high-crime urban settings nation-wide.

SECONDARY CONCLUSIONS. The Report also reaches several secondary conclusions:

Institutional Settings. Most crime prevention results from informal and formal practices and programs located in seven institutional settings. These institutions appear to be "interdependent" at the local level, in that events in one of these institution can affect events in others that in turn can affect the local crime rate. These are the seven institutions identified in Chapter Two [of the report]:

- Communities
- Families
- Schools
- Labor Markets
- Places (specific premises)
- Police
- Criminal Justice

Effective Crime Prevention in High-Violence Neighborhoods May Require Interventions in Many Local Institutions Simultaneously. The interdependency of these local institutions suggests a great need for rigorous testing of programs that simultaneously invest in communities, families, schools, labor markets, place security, police and criminal justice. Operation Weed and Seed provides the best current example of that approach, but receives a tiny fraction of DOJ funding.

Crime Prevention Defined. Crime prevention is defined not by intentions or methods, but by results. There is scientific evidence, for example, that both schools and prisons can help prevent crime. Crime prevention programs are neither "hard" nor "soft" by definition; the central question is whether any program or institutional practice results in fewer criminal events than would otherwise occur. Chapter Two presents this analysis.

The Effectiveness of Federal Funding Programs. The likely impact of federal funding on crime and its risk factors, especially youth violence, can only be assessed using scientifically recognized standards in the context of what is known about each of the seven institutions. Chapter One [of the full report] presents the scientific basis for this conclusion. Each of the chapters on the seven institutional settings concludes with an analysis of the implications of the scientific findings for the likely effectiveness of the Department of Justice Programs.

What Works in Each Institution. The available evidence does support some conclusions about what works, what doesn't, and what's promising in each of the seven institutional settings for crime prevention. These conclusions are reported at the end of each of Chapters 3-9 [of the full report]. In order to reach these conclusions, however, the Report uses a relatively low threshold of the strength of scientific evidence. This threshold is **far lower than ideal** for informing Congressional decisions about billions of dollars in annual appropriations, and reflect the limitations of the available evidence.

Stronger Evaluations. The number and strength of available evaluations is insufficient for providing adequate guidance to the national effort to reduce serious crime. This knowledge gap can only be filled by Congressional restructuring of the DOJ programs to provide adequate scientific controls for careful testing of program effectiveness. DOJ officials currently lack the authority and funding for strong evaluations of efforts to reduce serious violence.

Statutory Evaluation Plan. In order to provide the Department of Justice with the necessary scientific tools for program evaluations, the statutory plan for evaluating crime prevention requires substantial revision. Scientifically recognized standards for program evaluations require strong controls over the allocation of program funding, in close coordination with the collection of relevant data on the content and outcomes of the programs. The current statutory plan does not permit the necessary level of either scientific controls on program operations or coordination with data collection. Funds available for data collection have also been grossly inadequate in relation to scientific standards for measurement of program impact.

Chapter Ten [of the full report] presents a statutory plan for accomplishing the Congressional mandate to evaluate with these elements:

1. **Earmark ten percent of all DOJ funding of local assistance for crime prevention (as defined in this Report) for operational program funds to be controlled by a central evaluation office within OJP.**

2. **Authorize the central evaluation office to distribute the ten percent "evaluated program" funds on the sole criteria of producing rigorous scientific impact evaluations, the results of which can be generalized to other locations nationwide.** Allocating these funds for field testing purposes simply adds to the total funding for which any local jurisdiction is eligible. Thus the "evaluated program" funding becomes an additional incentive to cooperate with the scientific evaluation plan on a totally voluntary basis.

3. **Set aside an additional ten percent of all DOJ funding of local assistance for crime prevention to support the conduct of scientific evaluations by the central evaluation office.** This recommendation makes clear the true expense of using rigorous scientific methods to evaluate program impact. Victimization interviews, offender self-reported offending, systematic observation of high crime locations, observations of citizen-police interaction, and other methods can all cost as much or more than the program being evaluated.

DEPARTMENT OF JUSTICE FUNDING FOR LOCAL CRIME PREVENTION

Chapter One [of the full report] describes the basic structure and mechanisms for Department of Justice FY 1996 funding of State and local governments and communities for assistance in crime prevention. The two major categories are $1.4 billion in funding of local police by the Office for Community-Oriented Policing Services (COPS), and $1.8 billion in local crime prevention assistance funding of a wide range of institutions by the Office for Justice Programs (OJP).[11] This review examines both the relatively small funding for **discretionary** grants by DOJ, many of which are determined by Congressional "earmarks" to

particular grantees and programs, and **formula** grants, which are distributed to State or local governments based on statutory criteria such as population size or violent crimes.

These are the principal OJP offices administering both types of grants: the Bureau of Justice Assistance administers the $503 million Local Law Enforcement Block Grants, the $475 million Byrne Formula Grants, and the $32 Million in Byrne Discretionary Grants; the Office of Juvenile Justice and Delinquency Prevention administers the $70 Million Juvenile Justice Formula Grants, and the $69 Million Competitive Grants; the Violence Against Women Grants Office administers the $130 Million STOP Violence Against Women Formula Grants and $28 Million in Discretionary Grants To Encourage Arrests; Corrections Program Office administers a $405 Million Formula Grants for prison construction and a $27 Million Grants Program for substance abuse treatment of prison inmates; the Drug Courts Program Office funds $15 Million (from LLEBG) to local drug courts. The Executive Office of Weed and Seed administers the $28 Million (from Byrne) Federal component of the Weed and Seed Program in selected high-crime inner-city areas.

SCIENTIFIC STANDARDS FOR PROGRAM EVALUATIONS

The Omnibus Crime Control and Safe Streets Act of 1968 defines an "evaluation" as "the administration and conduct of studies and analyses to determine the impact and value of a project or program in accomplishing the statutory objectives of this chapter."[12] By this definition, an evaluation cannot be only a description of the implementation process, or "monitoring" or "auditing" the expenditure of the funds. Such studies can be very useful for many purposes, including learning how to implement programs. But they cannot show whether a program has succeeded in causing less crime, and if so by what magnitude. Nor can the results be easily generalized.

The scientific standards for inferring causation have been clearly established and have been used in other Reports to the Congress to evaluate the strength of evidence included in each program evaluation. With some variations in each setting, the authors of the present Report use an adapted version of scoring system employed in the 1995 National Structured Evaluation by the Center for Substance Abuse Prevention. The system is used to rate available evaluations on a "scientific methods score" of 1 through 5. The scores generally reflect the level of confidence we can place in the evaluation's conclusions about cause and effect. Chapter Two describes the specific procedures followed in the application of this 1–5 rating system, as well as its limitations.

DECIDING WHAT WORKS

The scientific methods scores reflect only the strength of evidence about program effects on crime, and not the strength of the **effects** themselves. Due to the general weakness of the available evidence, the Report does not employ a standard method of rating programs according to the magnitude of their effect size. It focuses on the prior question of whether there is reasonable certainty that a program has any beneficial effect at all in preventing crime. The limitations of the available evidence for making this classification are discussed in Chapter Two [of the full report]. We note these limitations as we respond to the mandate for this Report and classify major local crime prevention practices in each institutional setting as follows:

What Works. These are programs that we are reasonably certain prevent crime or reduce risk factors for crime in the kinds of social contexts in which they have been evaluated, and for which the findings should be generalizable to similar settings in other places and times. Programs coded as "working" by this definition must have at least two level 3 evaluations with statistical significance tests **and** the preponderance of all available evidence showing effectiveness.

What Doesn't Work. These are programs that we are reasonably certain **fail** to prevent crime or reduce risk factors for crime, using the identical scientific criteria used for deciding what works.

What's Promising. These are programs for which the level of certainty from available evidence is too low to support generalizable conclusions, but for which there is some empirical basis for predicting that further research could support such conclusions. Programs are coded as "promising" if they found effective in at least one level 3 evaluation **and** the preponderance of the evidence.

What's Unknown. Any program not classified in one of the three above categories is defined as having unknown effects.

EFFECTIVENESS OF LOCAL CRIME PREVENTION PRACTICES

The scientific evidence reviewed focuses on the local crime prevention practices that are supported by both federal and local, public and private resources. Conclusions about the scientifically tested effectiveness of these practices are organized by the seven local institutional settings in which these practices operate.

Chapter 3: Community-Based Crime Prevention reviews evaluations of such practices as community organizing and mobilization against crime, gang violence prevention, community-based mentoring, and after-school recreation programs.

Chapter 4: Family-Based Crime Prevention reviews evaluations of such practices as home visitation of families with infants, preschool education programs involving parents, parent training for managing troublesome children, and programs for preventing family violence, including battered women's shelters and criminal justice programs.

Chapter 5: School-Based Prevention reviews evaluations of such practices as DARE, peer-group counseling, gang resistance education, anti-bullying campaigns, law-related education, and programs to improve school discipline and improve social problem-solving skills.

Chapter 6: Labor Markets and Crime Risk Factors reviews evaluations of the crime prevention effects of training and placement programs for unemployed people, including Job Corps, vocational training for prison inmates, diversion from court to employment placements, and transportation of inner-city residents to suburban jobs.

Chapter 7: Preventing Crime At Places reviews the available evidence on the effectiveness of practices to block opportunities for crime at specific locations like stores, apartment buildings and parking lots, including such measures as cameras, lighting, guards and alarms.

Chapter 8: Policing For Crime Prevention reviews evaluations of such police practices as directed patrol in crime hot spots, rapid response time, foot patrol, neighborhood watch, drug raids, and domestic violence crackdowns.

Chapter 9: Criminal Justice and Crime Prevention reviews the evidence on such practices as prisoner rehabilitation, mandatory drug treatment for convicts, boot camps, shock incarceration, intensively supervised parole and probation, home confinement and electronic monitoring.

EFFECTIVENESS OF DEPARTMENT OF JUSTICE FUNDING PROGRAMS

DOJ funding supports a wide range of practices in all seven institutional settings, although much more so in some than in others. Congress has invested DOJ funding most heavily in police and prisons, with very little support for the other institutions. The empirical and theoretical evidence shows that other settings for crime prevention are also important, especially in the small number of urban neighborhoods with high rates of youth violence. Thus the statutory allocation of investments in the crime prevention "portfolio" is lop-sided, and may be missing out on some major dividends.

The effectiveness of existing DOJ funding mechanisms is assessed at the end of each chapter [of the full report] on local crime prevention practices...

CONCLUSION

The great strength of federal funding of local crime prevention is the innovative strategies it can prompt in cities like New York, Boston, and Kansas City (MO) where substantial reductions have recently occurred in homicide and youth violence. The current limitation of that funding, however, is that it does not allow the nation to learn **why** some innovations work, exactly **what** was done, and **how** they can be successfully adapted in other cities. In short, the current statutory plan does not allow DOJ to provide effective guidance to the nation about what works to prevent crime.

Yet despite the current limitations, DOJ has clearly demonstrated the contribution it can make by increasing such knowledge. The Department has already provided far better guidance to State and local governments on the effectiveness of all local crime prevention efforts than was available even a decade ago. Based on the record to date, only DOJ agencies, and not the State and local governments, have the available resources and expertise to produce the kind of generalizable conclusions Congress asked for in this report. The statutory plan this report recommends would enhance that role, and allow DOJ to accomplish the longstanding Congressional mandate to find generally effective programs to combat serious youth violence. By focusing that effort in the concentrated poverty areas where most serious crime occurs, the Congress may enable DOJ to reverse the epidemic of violent crime that has plagued the nation for three decades.

NOTES

1. Laurie Asseo, "Inmate Lawsuits," The Associated Press on-line, May 24, 1996.

2. See, for example, "The Great Prison Pastime," 20/20, ABC News, September 24, 1993, which is part of the video library available to instructor's using *Criminal Justice Today*.

3. Ibid.

4. "Inmate Lawsuits."

5. Public Law 104–134. Although the PLRA was signed into law on April 26, 1996, and is frequently referred to as the "Prison Litigation Reform Act of 1996," the official name of the act is the "Prison Litigation Reform Act of 1995."

6. Ibid.

7. Ibid.

8. "Inmate Litigation and the PLRA," *Corrections Compendium,* December, 1996, p. 2.

9. Randall Mikkelsen, "U.S. 'Cybersmut' Suit Gives Glimpse of Internet Future," Reuters wire service, March 21, 1996.

10. Randall Mikkelsen, "U.S. Court Blocks New Internet-Indecency Law," Reuters wire service, June 12, 1996.

11. Total FY 1996 funding for the Office of Justice Programs was $2.7 billion, including $228 Million in collections for the Office for Victims of Crime.

12. 42 U.S.C. Section 3791 (10).